WHY MEN CHEAT?

WHY MEN CHEAT?

Toris Jones

PRIMIX
PUBLISHING
THE WRITE CHOICE

Primix Publishing
11620 Wilshire Blvd
Suite 900, West Wilshire Center, Los Angeles, CA, 90025
www.primixpublishing.com
Phone: 1-800-538-5788

Published by Primix Publishing: 04/10/2024

ISBN: 979-8-89194-135-9(sc)
ISBN: 979-8-89194-136-6(e)

Library of Congress Control Number: 2024905367

Contents

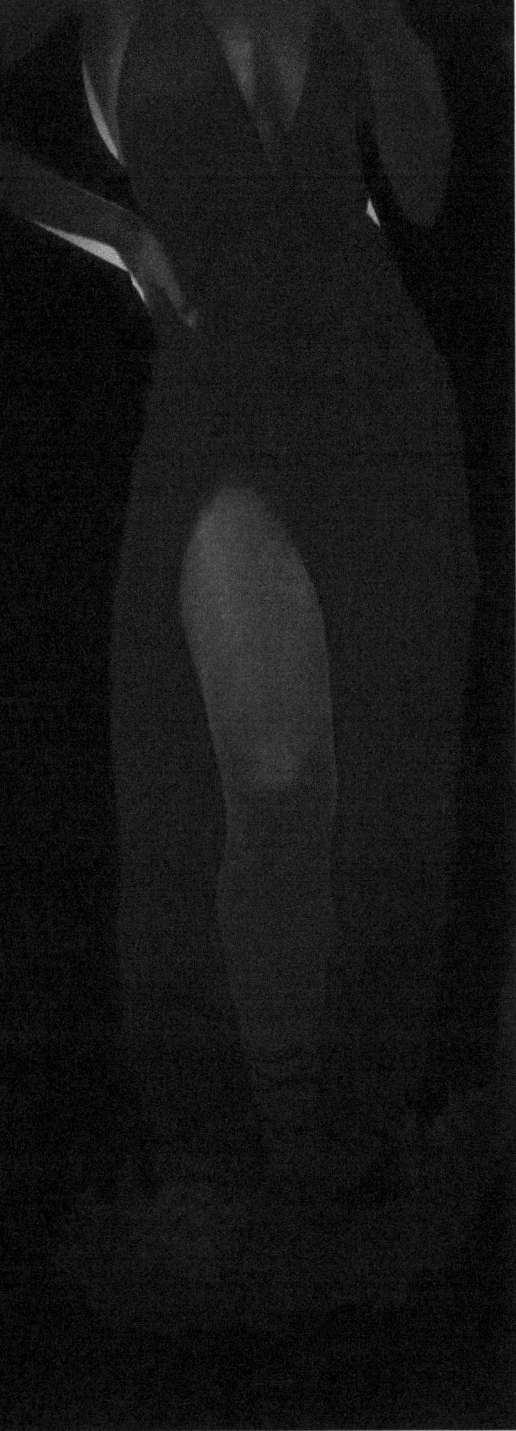

For All Man Kind

SPECIAL CHEMICAL WE USED IN THE MOLECULAR FOUNDRY LAB. I KNEW NOW THAT WHAT I'D DONE TO LAWRENCE
DO AGAIN—AND THAT I COULD EVEN CONTROL IT. AT LEAST WHILE WE WERE IN THE BACK OF THE POLICE
WITH EVAPORATING THINGS, TRYING TO MELT THE PLASTIC CUFF PINCHING MY WRISTS. I CONCENTRATED ON THE
BONDS HOLDING THEM TOGETHER, TRYING TO REPRODUCE THE FEELING I'D HAD JUST BEFORE THE SUV DISPERSED. IN
MY ARMS WERE FREE, THOUGH BRIEFLY WET. AT THE STATION, ALL OF US WERE PROCESSED AND RELEASED. IT TURN
HAD SOME KIND OF TRUST FUND THAT INVOLVED LAWYERS AND LOTS OF MONEY TO SPEND ON BAILING OUT HER AC
WHENEVER THEY GOT INTO TROUBLE. THE GREEN LIBERATION ARMY WASTED NO TIME TURNING ME INTO THEIR CITIZ
THE ECO-AVENGER. ORDINARY PEOPLE WHO DRESSED IN COSTUMES TO FIGHT CRIME WERE ALL THE RAGE THAT YEAR
OF THE TV SERIES WHO WANTS TO BE A SUPERHERO? BUT MOST OF THE CITIZEN SUPERHERO VIDEOS WERE JUST EMB
GUYS IN MASKS AND MOTORCYCLE JACKETS YELLING AT POT DEALERS IN SUBURBAN PARKS. MARIA GOT ME SOME GRE
AND A SKI MASK, AND FILMED WHILE I EVAPORATED CARS. SHE ADDED LITTLE COMIC BOOK BUBBLES TO THE VIDEOS
THINGS LIKE "TAKE THAT, ENVIRONMENT-DESTROYING GAS GUZZLER!" OR "ONCE AGAIN, ECO-AVENGER SAVES THE W
THE CAR MENACE!" SHE POSTED ON CITIZEN SUPERHERO WEBSITES AND GOT HER FRIENDS AT THE ENVIRONMENTAL
BLOG TO DO A STORY ABOUT OUR WORK. EVENTUALLY BOINGBOING LINKED TO ONE OF THE VIDEOS, PROCLAIMING M
CITIZEN SUPERHERO ON THE WEB, "BECAUSE THE SPECIAL EFFECTS ARE SO GOOD THAT IT REALLY LOOKS LIKE THE ECO
HAS A SUPERPOWER!" EVERY TIME I RAN MY HANDS OVER AN SUV AND FELT ITS ELECTRONS UNZIP, I HAD MORE QUE
WAS ALL THIS DISAPPEARED MASS GOING? YOU'D EXPECT THE DEMOLISHED MOLECULAR BONDS TO RELEASE ENOUGH
TO THROW ME ACROSS THE ROOM, OR EXPLODE, BUT INSTEAD THERE WAS ONLY A COOL MIST. MAYBE MY POWER WA
FOR DEMOLITION. I COMBED THE WEB FOR STORIES OF CARS THAT HAD MATERIALIZED OUT OF NOWHERE AND FOUN
MY WORKING THEORY WAS THAT MY POWERS OF DESTRUCTION SEEMED TO AFFECT BOTH MASS AND ENERGY. IN
WEIRD KIND OF ... BUT DIDN'T GET ME ANY CLOSER TO FIGURING OUT WHAT HAD HAPPENED TO LAWRENCE. I EN
DEG ... AND TO A RESEARCH JOB AT THE MOLECULAR FOUNDRY, CHURNING ... INVISIBLE SHELFS OF CARB ...
IN CHARGE OF THE LAB MARVELED AT MY DEDICATION TO THE JOB. MY DEDICATION
... OLD ... SUBSTRATE, BUT IT WAS ALL SELF-SERVING. I WA ... REVERSE ENGINEER I CONTINUED MOVING
TARGET OBJECTS WITH AN EXTREME DEGREE OF GRANULAR ... HELPFUL ... AT ... BE
... THOSE EXPERIMENTS WEREN'T PARTICULARLY ... WHAT I WAS DOING, WHO KNEW WHAT ... THE
AND JUST MAYBE REGENERATE. AT LAST, EACH ... ONE ... CAN
NOTUBE. I GOT SO EXCITED THAT IT PUFFED OUT OF EXISTENCE ... REPEATE
... INGLY AWAY ... OD OF MONTHS. I BEGAN TO WORK ON MORE ... CATED OBJECTS, CONJURING BLOO
... AIR AND LUNG TISSUE ... OF SALT. WHEN I FELT A SOLID OBJECT CURL ... OUT OF THE ATOMS IN MY HANDS, I MA
... SUBSTANCE COMING FROM ... EVERYTHING I HAD TAKEN APART AND SENT WHIRLING INTO SUBATOMIC SPACE, ALL THE
HAD DISAPPEARED WAS COMING BACK TO ME. IN SPRING, I RETURNED TO THE TOWN WHERE LAWRENCE AND I GREW
AGO, ALMOST TO THE WEEK, I HAD REDUCED LAWRENCE TO VAPOR. NOW I WOULD USE MY POWERS TO REBUILD HI
SUBATOMIC PARTICLES HE'D LEFT BETWEEN THOSE TWO TRASH BINS. THE CRATER HAD BEEN FILLED IN WITH NEW ...
AGO, AND THE DONUT SHOP WAS GONE. IT DIDN'T MATTER. I STOOD IN THE MIDDLE OF THE PARKING LOT, FEELING E
THAT MOVED THROUGH ME, CLOSING MY EYES, I EXTENDED MY ARMS AND REMEMBERED HOW IT FELT TO RUN ... FIN
LAWRENCE'S BODY. HIS HAIR WAS THICK, HIS COLLARBONE SHARP, VEINS RAN IN SOFT BULGES DOWN HIS INNER ARM
HIS MUSCLES WERE ALWAYS BUNCHED INTO HYPERVIGILANCE. I TASTED HIM IN MY MOUTH, TRANSLATED PHOTONS
AT FIRST IT WAS UNCERTAIN, BUT THEN I COULD FEEL THE SHREDS OF HIS MOLECULAR STRUCTURE ARRIVING, GROWIN
OUT OF NOTHING INTO MY WAITING HANDS. THE AIR GREW CLOUDY WITH HIS ASSEMBLING TISSUE. IT WAS FIRST
WAS EMERGING NAKED, WET SOLIDITY. JUST AS I COULD SEE THE OUTLINE OF HIS FACE, HE EXPLODED, COLLAP
A COOLING SOLID WHICH I COULD BARELY CONTROL. THERE WAS ONLY ONE THING I COULD DO IF I WANTED TO KEEP
HAD CONJURED FROM DISPERSING. EXTEMPORIZE. I GATHERED WHAT REMAINED OF HIM BETWEEN THE PARENTHESE
HANDS, SQUEEZING HIS PARTICLES INTO AN ULTRA-DENSE TORUS. WHAT CLANGED ... TO THE GROUND LOOKED EXACT
OLD WEDDING BAND. LAWRENCE COULD FIT ON MY RING FINGER, BUT HE WEIGHED ... AS MUCH AS HE HAD IN LIFE. IT
THING, DRAGGING HIM HOME. I BROUGHT LAWRENCE TO WORK INSIDE A REINFORCED STEEL BOX THAT FITTED ONTO
HAD A LOT OF CRAZY IDEAS, THOUGHTS ABOUT HOW I COULD REBUILD HIM. MAYBE I COULD BURY HIM, AND GROW
OUT OF THE MINERAL-RICH EARTH. OR BRING HIM TO THE TISSUE ENGINEERING LAB, AND TRY TO SITUATE HIM IN
EXISTING FLESH? I WAS CONTEMPLATING THESE POSSIBILITIES WHEN MARIA SENT ME A TEXT. SHE WAS MOVING TO
ON A FEATURE, AND TONIGHT WOULD BE OUR LAST CAR DISINTEGRATION VIDEO. "CAN U MEET AT SHIPYARDS B4 LIGH
OUT?" SHE ASKED. I COULD. WHEN I ARRIVED, PULLING LAWRENCE BEHIND ME, SHE WAS THE ONLY PERSON THERE
MEMBERS OF THE GREEN LIBERATION ARMY WERE APPARENTLY BUSY AT THEIR OFFICE JOBS. MARIA WAS LEANING AG
BRAND-NEW RAV4, EATING SALAD OUT OF A PLASTIC YOGURT CONTAINER. "DO YOU THINK YOU COULD MAKE THIS C
WHILE IT'S MOVING?" SHE ASKED. "IT WOULD LOOK SO COOL TO SHOW THE CAR ROTTING FROM THE INSIDE OUT. I COU
THE CAMERA ON THE DASHBOARD AND FILM THE WHOLE THING WHILE DRIVING." AS MARIA EXPLAINED THE SETUP
BLOCKED OUT EACH SHOT WITH HER HANDS. I WAS GOING TO MISS TALKING OPENLY TO SOMEBODY ABOUT VAPORIZ
MARIA DIDN'T KNOW THAT MY POWER CAME FROM SOMETHING BEYOND THE UNDERSTANDING OF SCIENCE, BUT SHE
USE IT MORE TIMES THAN ANYONE. AND UNTIL TODAY, SHE'D ALWAYS WANTED MORE. BEFORE I COULD LOSE MY NER
MY HANDS ON HER BARE ARMS AND KISSED HER ON THE MOUTH. "IF THIS IS OUR LAST VIDEO, LET'S REALLY MAKE IT
SAID. SHE DIDN'T LOOK SURPRISED. WE OPENED THE HATCHBACK AND PULLED OURSELVES INSIDE. I HOISTED LAWRE
IN BEHIND US, THE HANDCART BANGING OVER THE BUMPER. SOMEHOW WE WORMED OUT OF OUR CLOTHES IN THE
SPACE. AS I KISSED HER NECK, I THOUGHT ABOUT HOW ALL HUMAN SKIN FEELS MORE OR LESS THE SAME, BODIES AN
IF YOU CONSIDER THEM FROM THE PERSPECTIVE OF VERY SMALL SURFACE AREAS. I STRADDLED HER AND LISTENED TO
OF OUR BREATHING. THE WINDOWS BEGAN TO FOG UP AND I GRABBED THE BOX TO HOLD MYSELF STEADY. IT POPPE
LAWRENCE ROLLED OUT, COMING TO REST NEXT TO HER SHOULDER. MAYBE THIS WAS WHAT I'D WANTED ALL ALONG
THE RING AND LAWRENCE STREAMED THROUGH ME, REPLACING EVERY MOLECULE IN HER BODY WITH ONE OF HIS. I CO
STOP. I WAS POURING HIM INTO HER. MARIA'S EYES FADED TO DARK AND HER CHEST BROADENED. SQUIRMING AND
SHE HOVERED IN A VAGUE SPACE BETWEEN HERSELF AND LAWRENCE. I COULD SEE EVERY OUTLINE OF HIS BODY IN

Love Jones

I Got A Story To Tell

Welcome Address

To all of us men around the world, I took time out to write this book "*Why Men Cheat*". In writing this book, I'm not encouraging one of you to cheat. However, I'm sharing with you all, how I ended up cheating. The question I would like to ask is "*Why*" are there excuses? For you know or should I say, you should know what led you to cheat and it wasn't because you argued with your lady, it surely isn't because she cooked the same dish tonight as she did last night. You have watched too many fictional movies fella…. So, stop with that! There is a reason and a lot of us deal with it daily. Let's get to it.

All Man Kind

If one were to tell me a certain Race doesn't cheat, He probably woke up this morning beating his meat.

There his wife lay in bed in the bedroom talking about cheating in the next room. Well there you go!

We all are guilty
no ands, if's and buts
about it.

C-mon you know you weren't busting off to your significant other.

Animalistic Behavior

I was watching T.V. a few days ago, on my T.V. was Animal Planet, it was an episode about Meerkats. A Meerkat is a Mongoose found in Southern Africa. The couple can produce two to four pups a year. So, I see the Meerkat standing on his hind legs and tail protecting his family of four, with his chest sticking out looking out for predators and rival gangs, Snakes, Hawks, Eagles, and Jackals to name a few. I saw where the Meerkat killed a King Cobra, I also saw a Meerkat pull a stinger off a scorpion and start eating it. The male Meerkat was doing everything to provide for his family, I was fascinated looking at how proud and dominant the Male Meerkat was. I saw where other Meerkat groups would watch out for others while some of the males would go hunting for food for the family. Well while hunting, the male Meerkat I'm sure never thought his female companion would've done him and the kids wrong while hunting and working for the family. The male Meerkat looks up standing on his hind legs and sees his female companion the mother of his kids having sexual relations with another. To make matters worse she was making out in front of the kids, she was giving the goods to a rival gang, I'm sure it didn't matter who it was to the proud father, I was done looking at this! I was interested in the male Meerkat's next move! The proud father took off running home to check the filth his lady and mother of his children was displaying before his eyes. The rival Meerkat was getting down and dirty with the proud father Meerkat's wife, He took off running when he saw the proud father coming. His wife was jumpy and edgy fussing and cussing, I guess. The proud father wasn't trying to hear anything she had to say, he ran her off with the rival gang Meerkat, she wasn't trying to leave, but the proud father left her no choice, but to leave. The mother meerkat went on her way leaving behind her kids. This was the part of the T.V. showing of the Meerkats that had me in Awe! When the rival gang Meerkat went back home on his turf or community if you will, I guess he told his gang what had just happened and they all took off running to go get at the proud father, at that point the mother was with the rival gang. The proud father sensed something was coming and that he may have to go to war, truly he sniffed it out he was right, and trouble arrived. The proud father was already prepared with his gang again standing with his chest out. They had a face-off, I guess the rival gang figured they were outnumbered because they surely retreated. The rival gang probably thought they were ready for war until they stared war in the face. The proud father wasn't having any of that, standing in front of his gang in his community. After a day of hard work earning pay for the family, you come home to see your lady at play with another. This may have happened to some of you fellas out there. I've never been through that, but I can only imagine the hurt and pain. Some women may be offended after reading this, but if this isn't you...Why would it offend you, simply put the book down and STOP reading it, because it only gets better, maybe it's you who needs to take a look in the mirror, it's not always the man at fault. Salute to the Meerkat I'm sure a lot of us men would've done the same. If not, I guess you have your reason. But one would question "Why Men Cheat".

F.Y.I.

For we men have been called every bad name there is. What I would like to know is why are so many mad at us men. Is it because you're not a man because that's the only way you'll know who we are? Is it because we men were put here on earth before the woman? I have many questions I can ask but I assure you theirs not enough paper in the world to write every woman's answer that they would come up with. You might hear one say, I'm sick and tired of dating, all men are the same! I'm here to let you know you're far from the truth and you 40+ and you still haven't figured that out or are you just in love with "Trying" to bring us down because we real men stand 10 toes down no matter what the foolish people today say. If there's something you don't like, it's you or the person you attracted (to) change… So, change it up sweetheart trust me real love is out there. This applies to us men as well, if you keep getting hurt over and over by your culture try another race, it's not saying you're turning your back on your race, but you've endured too much hurt to try again. No matter who approves or not, your mom your dad your kids, siblings, and friends who care. You must live your life for you besides, The Creator is Love and I've never read anywhere in the Holy Bible where it says you need to date your race only. This comes from a place of ignorance because The Creator loves his people for, he created us all. Somebody has to explain why they're single, someone is telling a friend or a family member right now how foul your now ex is, but yet you result to the same again only to hurt again, sometimes two can get lucky or blessed I like to say and it works out it doesn't mean they don't go through some trials, because just as sure as you live you will go through some ups and downs and if you haven't, you haven't lived long enough. I'm talking to the rich and the poor and the middle class as they call it. Anyways…A lot of the people who talk that kind of foolishness about race are the ones who are single or in a relationship and possibly may even be cheating with someone from another race, or they may want to give interracial relations a try, but like I said or mentioned earlier they're just scared of what one may say. Why would you listen to anyone who's not happy with themselves, they've never dated outside of their race, simply again I say that's coming from a place of ignorance. Also, how can one speak about a thing and never experienced it, not unless they've tried it and now, they've been exploited, how can you talk about an experience you've never had, like I said not unless they have and now they're "Busted". But again, this is the person you're listening to. You may have missed out on what could have been love, well just keep on listening to hurt people. How can they help you when they're hurt... I know ... I know !!! They can't, both of you are on crutches because you chose to be. I know one thing for sure, if I'm stuck in a ditch and slipping away, I wouldn't care what race they are as long as they pull me out to safety, and if you disagree then truly you need some help, so cut all the foolishness with the racism. No matter how much I say these things some people think Hell won't be so bad, I tell you what flick a cigarette lighter or strike a match and hold your hand over the flame, well F.Y.I. read the book of "Revelations" and read where it talks about how hot the fire is and how you'll be tormented forever your soul that is. A lot of you have put up with what you'll call Hell on Earth, I dare you to read "Revelations" and act as if it doesn't shake you up a bit. You may think you want to go to hell, but what you have gone through here on Earth won't be anything close to hell. How I know well I'm a believer in God's word and the word can't lie and won't lie. You on the other hand need to change your heart and "STOP" with hate and hellish ways and outlooks. Is it fate you ended up in a ditch you know warning comes before destruction, F.Y.I., I don't like arguing with a fool, I don't like arguing period, but arguing with a fool hits a bit differently. Be prepared not surprised.

Bust A Nut

Well, she said tonight is the night she'll make it alright just come over. I said no, no now I can't do such a thing. She said underneath this skirt I have on a cherry red thong, Damn I'll be wrong. She said would you like to see? I said ugh no. She said my fancy is wet, what are you gonna do about it? I said nothing She said you know you can have this fancy however which way you want it! I want you to hit it until the morning. Can you do that she softly said? Playing with herself, she said my fancy is smelling like strawberries, come help me produce the cream, let's make this dream reality, I'm so horny she bends over and moaned you can hit this fancy from Carolina to California. Stop acting as if you don't want this she said. So, what you gonna do when the ass is phat and a chest to match, know how to work the hips, the lips as well, she said tell me, don't you want to put that scented lotion on my plush bottom come back and do the same shit tomorrow! No strings attached tell me are you feeling that? I said no, no I'm gone got home, and my lady, period on… Damn!! Dick hard aww the odd job. I got in the shower and thought about the plush bottom in the skirt in a matter of minutes, I busted a nut. Well, now I guess I'm wrong, for I'm weak a little bitter all in all I'm a cheater.

True Story,
By Toris Jones

Why Men Cheat

Here I stand well over 5ft just an inch south of 6ft, 235 lbs. of muscle with an athletic build. I'm proud of the Brown pigmentation I don, just as handsome as I could be humbly, I say although I may not be handsome to some of the ladies and that's ok, I'm not for everybody and everybody isn't for me. I'm secure with myself! I feel good about the man I am, and I hope all feel good and confident about who you are. I'm an Alpha Male for sure! If you're not confident about who you are maybe after reading this book you will be. What do you call a happy home? You and I may have different outlooks of what a happy home is. I was always told happy wife and a happy life, but how about us men do we not deserve happiness? I can do the world for my sweetheart, and she could be doing the world for me as well. Sometimes she does. She cooks that good food, and the dessert has me wanting more and more she's some kind of wonderful, she's as fine as frog hair. With a curve like a tractor-trailer steering wheel, I'm telling you something real LOL.... No lie for theirs some things that we all can work on in relationships no one has it all together, but, yet we make it work. I spoil her she spoils me; you don't have to be extremely paid if you get paid, and you bring in a legal income. And if you're not content with your wages then changes need to be made. Don't go putting each other down especially if one is doing their best if anything support your significant other don't be looking down your nose, because you earn more money, I heard a wise man say, that when you making your way up that pole, you better grease it, because it's going to hurt when you fall. Treating people badly will cause you to fall a bit faster. Reality has it that sometimes we outgrow each other, simply because some have reached their zenith, if this is some of you then "split happens", I understand especially time after time you've had the conversation and they say they're going to change, but they remain stagnant. Get out of there I encourage you. At that point, you two are oil and water and we all know oil and water don't mix. Again, get out of there and I do mean fast, and don't look back. For how many years must repeat the same thing, what's understood doesn't have to be explained. I start my day by thanking The Creator first and foremost. Eat breakfast, I check the mirror to make sure the confirmation says TJ, I approve. Then I'm off to work. My employer is filled with ladies every time I look up there's a woman or women in my face and the field of Pharmaceuticals woo wee, I'm talking about all ethnicities. No disrespect to all the lovelies! Let's go.... A lot of us men come up with all kinds of reasons to cheat, when it comes to cheating on your mate there's only one reason. Your significant other may be the love of your life, well she may think so. Honestly speaking, you very well may love her, well if you do what is it that comes and tears you two apart? Here's my story, Here I am trying my best to be at my best. There comes a time in life when you'll be tested and trust me if you're doing good for yourself, then you'll be tested more. Throughout your life, how many tests have you taken? Now, ask yourself how many times did you fail? Pop quizzes are also included, be honest with yourself. If you're not honest with yourself, you've already failed. So, TJ I was told you do all types of artwork. Well, who told you that Lori? People talk you know, so do you? There are so many forms of art, so can you be a bit more specific? Lori shrugged her shoulders and said ooh-oh ugh…. I'm talking about you drawing a picture for me. I said Lori what type of drawing, is there a particular medium? She said Well you're the artist! I then asked the question the picture you're talking what exactly is it that you want me to draw? She says oh…. I want you to draw me in the nude! I said Lori you want me to do a masterpiece of you in the nude! Lori said oh my God yes, a masterpiece of me in the nude! I saw how excited she was when I said masterpiece, it was almost like she hit a switch or something in the way her eyes flickered. So, I said Lori you do understand we're coworkers and I do have a lady, you understand that right? Lori said yes, and she went on to say, I saw the Mural you did for Michelle. I said yes, I did a Mural for her son's room. But you're asking me to do a piece of you in the nude, this is night and day what you're asking me, and besides Mrs. Michelle is happily married, and besides I'm not a homewrecker. Lori said listen we're both adults, I'm sure a man like you has seen a lot of naked women. Just act as if we don't work together and besides you tell me your price and

I'll compensate you even more how about that? I have another question to ask, she said what is your question? Where am I supposed to do such a job of such at? surely it can't happen where me and my lady lay our heads…. also, what would your man have to say about this masterpiece. I don't have time for any problems. Lori said TJ I'm a single lady! I have my own everything, so no need to worry about anything. I said to myself yeah you have your own everything, but no man. She looked as sweet and sexy as could be. I said to myself, TJ what are you getting yourself into? I gave her the number for the compensation and told her that I would perform the work in charcoal. Well, see I figured if I do it in charcoal it will be fast. The sooner I can start and finish the better I thought. She gave me her address, her phone number, and all, I told her to let me know when she wanted me to start, and Lori said when we get off work and shower up works for me. I laughed! I said Lori my supplies are at my home, and I got to have those to do the job and I could have sworn I heard her say not really. Lori said Friday after work would be fine with me, I told her I'll get back with her on that out of respect I wanted to check with my lady to see if she had any plans for us. Knowing I didn't have any plans for myself and my significant other Trish. Lori said cool just let me know. When I got home, I told my lady someone wanted me to do an art piece, at this point my lady and I had been together for 2 years, and she accompanied me a few times when I did a Mural at Mrs. Michelle's house, so she trusted me. I called Lori and told her we could lock in on Friday. Truly she was screaming on the phone as if she won a vacation package or something, I said to myself after hanging up the phone, TJ are you sure you want to do this job? You know some guys wouldn't have uttered a thought after looking at Lori, but my lady is my Trophy there's no other lady that can come close to her. I remember an old man telling me at a carwash…. He said Hey young man, so what you got a lady, but let me tell you something, there's no pussy like new pussy. He figured to tell me that because two ladies walked over and the one lady showed me so much interest, I told her I was in a relationship and the old man I guess called himself, giving me the game. He was bothered by me saying I had a girlfriend to the 2 ladies. Let's just say I heard the old man loud and clear. The entire workday Friday Lori seemed as if she was on a mission, the way she was dressed. She made other co-workers ask her what kind of plans you have tonight, there were some of the guys coming over to my workstation talking to me about how sexy Lori was and how lucky her boyfriend was. She had this sexy new hairstyle enhanced by her beautiful skin glistering with a skirt that exposed her every curve. Truly she would've made a weak preacher sin, easily a blind man's vision would've jump-started facts of life you know. There I was at my workstation, and she walked up behind me while I was sitting doing my job, she whispered are you ready for tonight, because I am. I smelled her fragrance before she made it over to me. That's saying a lot because I'm a fragrance man, I don some nice cologne and trust and believe I get complimented daily. I spun my chair around and whispered back to her that if the address you gave me was accurate, I'd be there. When Lori left my workstation, I was accompanied by not just a co-worker or colleague, but I considered Allen aka Al a friend of mine. My buddy Allen said what Lori talking about. I simply said Lori was just leaving for the day and she was just saying have a good weekend. Allen said huh… come on man you don't have to lie! if I didn't know any better, I would think you and Lori have something going on. He went on to say, but I know you're still with your lady. I said Allen, me letting go of my lady. I can't see it happening for the fact never will I see it happen. Never say never though. I told Allen although Lori had been making heads turn all day even her girlfriends were looking like Damn!!! I said Lori was dressed so sexy. Allen said I think it was extreme, I said how do you figure? He said you don't think she violated the company's dress policy; Oh, I see where you're going with it, but I told Allen, Lori was within the policy the skirt was to her knees now how the skirt was fitting her is the thing! But those are her curves though, extreme to me is a lady exposing her boobs or booty cheeks. Lori wasn't exposing either, if anything she shocked everyone, so I say it was shock value. Allen said you know what you're right, I never looked at it like that… But I'll be damn if she wasn't wearing that skirt, she did look nice I must admit it myself. Allen said TJ, seriously would you if you weren't in a relationship? I said, just looking at her yes of course who wouldn't? Allen said you don't even have to ask me! Just looking with the naked eye can get the better of any of us no one is exempt women included, I have you know in the Holy Bible if you will…. let me give you all the scripture with the verse…Matthew 5:28, But I say, anyone who even looks at a woman with lust has already committed adultery with her in his heart. How many of us are guilty of that every one of us here is guilty and is as wrong as two left shoes. When Lori whispered in my ear it seemed as if everyone was looking with curiosity Let me explain Jealousy is some serious shit, because of who you are, some people don't want to see you win at anything for the fact it wouldn't matter if you were dead to them, oh for sure two co-workers hated to see me coming through the door. These are dangerous people; my advice is to stay away from them. I felt both guy's hatred towards me. I'll say this much, there were quite a few of us going out for my Birthday this was the date 08/08/08. I heard someone ask one of those jealous guys are you going out with everyone to celebrate TJ's Birthday? I heard one of them say, 888 is not a date to be celebrating for anyone, he went to tell her that she shouldn't be celebrating it either. Envy will have some people going straight to hell, for I never did anything but be a child of God to all. They were so full of hate towards me that where he knew 3 6's was bad, but he wanted 888 to be bad. Well, to whom this may concern, here are some Biblical facts about the number 8, It reads number 8 encompasses new beginnings regeneration, and resurrection. The work of the Holy Spirit. No way I'm saying going out and partying is a representation of The Creator's word, but it's a justification of the number 8 for which I just so happen to be born on the 8th day of August which is the 8th month, if I was to give or should I say share the birth year some of you may hate me as well. This is just validation for me that The Creator knew what he was doing when he created me, I have you all know this as well, when I was born my, or my God is what I heard as a baby, why because I was born with a head full of grey hair. Some of you may think nothing of that, maybe you would see it differently if it was you. No way am I saying you're not special, because we all are, all I'm saying is the hate some people have for you may even scare you, but may The Creator bless those hating colleagues because continuously that's what The Creator does for me. That same co-worker the haters told not to go, was there celebrating my day and we all enjoyed my Birthday thanks to The Creator everyone made it home safely, we'll get back to my Birthday celebration a little later, but for now let's get back to Lori and the Masterpiece. I got off work and, on my way, home Trish and I had dinner from some good carry-out.

The Hibachi food was extra good that night. We kissed and I left to go and start on the masterpiece, I'm thinking about how sweet my lady is and why I haven't made her out to be my wife. I love her. I pull up to the address, gather my art supplies, and ring the doorbell, Lori greets me with a hug, and she says finally we can do this! Lori at this time was wearing a sexy see-through robe. She said I've Damn near finished the entire bottle of wine waiting for you. I said it's all good as long as the artwork turns out to be that masterpiece you want! Lori said TJ can I ask you a question, I said sure this is your house a lovely one might I say. She said thank you. I asked her what the question was again…As Lori gathered her words, she said what are your fantasies if you have any? I told her, I'm not into fantasies, but more so reality. She said I don't believe that! I'm sure you fantasize about something. Respectfully I said Well things have flashed in my mind here and there, but fantasizing isn't me. Why you asked is what I said? Well, I'm a woman and maybe it's a women's thing to fantasize. If I tell you my fantasy, I'm not sure how you'll react…. well, let's see, we're both adults try me! I recall saying that, but I was thinking please keep it professional. Lori said Well I tell you what… I cut her off and said let's get started with the Masterpiece and we can pick back up on that conversation during a break or something because it is getting later, she said sure. Lori grabbed my hand and escorted me to her bedroom. I can't lie, one couldn't help but notice her booty cheeks bounce up and down as I witnessed while she walked. TJ you can do this easy BOY!!!, you'll be able to pass the test be strong, hey man you got this! We're in the bedroom and she said TJ…. I need a favor. what do you need I said. Lori asked if I could put that scented lotion on her backside. I said sure, I put the lotion on her back LOL! Lori said I'm talking about my entire backside. Currently, she's not wearing anything but nude. I first thought about not doing it and as soon as I was about to say something…. she said you're doing a Masterpiece of me in the nude so cut it out. I rubbed the scented lotion on her booty and thighs feet as well, by her reactions one would've said she must think she was in the massage parlor, she was moaning and zoning out she said I love a man that has strong hands like yours oh my God she said! Lori said I could get used to this, but I ignored the fact that she said that. So, after she applied the lotion all over Lori's backside, she said…. How do you want me TJ? She struck a pose with her hands in front of her fancy which she was looking innocent for which I thought, that was the one, but she struck another pose with her booty exposing me as she looked back at me…. I said yes that's the one!! But then she positioned herself doggie style and I quickly disagreed with that pose. Why do you disagree with that position TJ is what Lori asked. I said Lori don't make me say…. let's just keep this professional and I said besides the second pose is the one, because it shows a woman that shows a woman that knows she's sexy and knows how to satisfy her Man. Lori said ooh! I like that let's get it started. I said I'm ready. I was 25 minutes into the drawing, and she asked if we could take a break, I said no problem everything is coming along quite well. I thought it was 25 minutes, but it was 48 minutes into the job because I remember saying to myself after looking at my watch, I'm doing pretty good to be 25 minutes in, but hey time flies when you're having fun is what they say right. Lori walked over and said may I take a peek, I responded, you sure you don't want to wait till it's done? She said Well I guess I can. Lori put on her robe and we walked into the kitchen again, she escorted me by grabbing my hand I simply followed her lead. Lori is full of good vibes and good energy so while taking a break Lori said TJ you said you have a lady, correct? I said you're right, yes, I do have a lady. she said is it your wife? I said no, not yet, but maybe one day I can mature to that for which you asked. Lori said TJ remember when I asked you about fantasies earlier. I said yes, I guess now is a good time to talk about your fantasies, at this time she's sipping her wine and eating strawberries. Lori said TJ, I'm just being honest with you, ok? I said I'm listening. Lori said the first day I saw you, I fantasized about you. I flashed a concerned look, and I responded what kind of fantasy? Lori said mmm mmm-mmm let me tell you in a sexy voice!!! I fucked you and it was fucking Awesome! She said I lost control of myself numerous times at work looking and fantasizing about you! Lori said honestly speaking she wasn't the only lady at our employer that said the same thing. She said I'm not embarrassed to say many times she had changed her panties. I said wow!!! I was somewhat speechless and anyone who knows me knows it's unusual for me to be speechless. I can't lie she had me tongue-tied. I'm thinking Damn! She spilled on the other ladies at our employer as well although she didn't mention any names. Lori said TJ the thing I want to know is what are you going to do about this fantasy and fantasies about you I've been having? Lori walked closely to me, and I smelled the wine and strawberry breath when she asked me again, TJ what are you going to do about my fantasy? I said Lori come on now I told you I was in a relationship, let's not go there, Lori took my hand and slowly started motioning my hand and my fingers to her modification. I didn't have any desire to feel her fancy, she introduced it to me. My Carolina Wood was doing just fine up until my hand met fancy wet. Truth be told we didn't even make it back to her bedroom we were getting it on right there on the kitchen floor. She got on top of me making such a mess on me. She's moaning calling my name you name it she revealed. We're both in a zone where so many positions were inflicted, I believe her with her fantasy talk because I can tell she was coming from a place of passion every time the juices flowed, and the facial expressions had a lot to say as well. One would've thought we were done, but I went to shower and after 4 minutes of showering entered Lori there, we were again getting it…. I lifted her putting her back up against the wall and she went on another ride, this one slippier than the first, well obviously it would be if you two were in the shower, yeah but this water came down from pink walls. After everything was done and over, she looked as if she just hit some sort of lottery! Maybe she did according to her fantasies. She did say in one of her fantasies we were Awesome, well there you go. You all decide, meanwhile, I'm thinking about what I have done. It's always that DUMB ASS thought that comes to mind afterward. I "never cheated on my lady "NEVER"! Oh, well ugh…. Because how can one categorize cheating yes, I've looked at a porno flick time or two and got the job done. But in some eyes, they don't view that as cheating again just go back to the Bible verse "Matthew" 5:28 and see doesn't that validate we all are cheaters? This is talking to you too, you idiots who don't think you're not part of this world, because you are! Again, no one is exempt. Only The Creator can judge me, so say what you feel you need to say, but it will never eclipse the truth. I believe in truth you believe the lie and that's where we are today… sad, I tell you. That's why the world is as chaotic as it is now, but judgment awaits us all or do it, and if you're against "TRUTH" then it's not going to be good for you, this is a fact, and if you don't know who "TRUTH" is… I encourage you to read the "Holy Bible", but I encourage all to look into the lost books. There you'll find all the answers to life and a lot of you people still don't believe. But I look to The Creator for guidance and answers, I can't speak for the world. Questions are asked by many people even about the Holy Bible and I can see why, people deserve to know the Truth. Many lies have been told, but the truth is surely out there. A tough crowd I tell you. I quickly put on my clothes and Lori requested one more time before I left. I wasn't hearing anything, I was just trying to make my exit, Lori started licking and sucking my neck, Lori grabbed my Carolina Wood, and started performing exotics on me. Excuse me for saying this, but I'm going to share with you something my dad shared with me. He said Son, every woman has a vagina, it's just one work hers a little different from the other. My, my, my was he right, but then I said wait a minute my parents have been married as long as I've been living and I'm just north of 45, my parents have been married 50 years my siblings and our kids and their kids recently celebrated my parents 50th. He must've had many experiences a time or two while being a young man. There are a lot of things my dad taught and told me when coming of age, He never said Son you'll "never" go through life without scars. He would say what doesn't kill you will make you stronger. He also said I been married to your mother for 50 years, and I still don't understand her. LOL! Surely, he was right although my mom said son while making out with the ladies.... TJ don't just put in on her put it on her real good! You add that with a smart hardworking, handsome man, you can anticipate many problems cause you going to have them Lord knows I have. After we did the naughty again, I took a quick wash up, this time I locked the bathroom door, I knew I had to get out of there. It was close to 2 in the morning 0200. Lori said to me when I got out of the bathroom, she said TJ you are addictive it's like I can't get enough of you, she said that's not fair. I said I'm sorry Lori, I must get going. Lori had a look that said please don't go, but me not waking up seeing my beautiful lady face. Huh, No chance! I got home of course took another shower, I saw my lady lying in bed she was in a deep sleep I remember kissing her before I prayed and went to sleep. I was greeted with a good morning when I woke up, Cole in my eyes, I felt as if I could go back to sleep some of the guys can relate, I think. I said good morning, Trish how are you feeling this morning? Trish responded I feel good she went on to say I need to be asking you, how are you feeling. I didn't even hear you when you got back! What time did you get back TJ? I said it was after two maybe around 0220. Trish said Well did you finish the job already? I said no there's still more work to be done. And fellas y'all know that Dumb ass look we have when we know we've done something we had "no" business doing. That was me 100%. We tell on ourselves in advance. Surely, we become paranoid with our thoughts, like does she know something that I don't know, however, we become extra nice to our significant other because we know we just comforted another lovely lady. At that point, if our ladies only knew, that they could get anything from us, but anyway. LOL…. No, I'm serious! Trish said Well TJ, I don't think coming in that late is going to work. Trish said can you work on coming home at a decent hour? Out of respect for my lady, I said no problem, sweetheart although I still had my own home, I could've just gone there. Anyway…. You all heard the saying it's a small world, well Trish and I went out to dinner late that Saturday evening, and sitting at another table who do I see??? You guessed it right if you said Lori. Lori was accompanied by some of her girlfriends one of them being one of our co-workers and her best friend. I said hello to them as my lady and I were seated. My lady said oh ok so you know them? I said yes. I only know two of them, there were four. I told Trish two of them were colleagues and before I was able to say anything Lori and Brandi decided to come and say hello. I introduced my lady to Lori and Brandi, they both said nice to meet you and Lori said TJ if you're not too busy tomorrow you think you can finish the art? I thought to myself Aww you can't be serious right now. I said it depends on my lady and how we feel after church service. Lori said no problem, I'll surely anticipate your call enjoy your dinners. My lady said so you're doing artwork for her. Yes, she's the one. Trish said she's pretty, she doesn't look better than me, but she is pretty. What was crazy and intense was when my lady went to the restroom, sitting across from me (Lori) started looking at me rubbing her fancy it didn't stop there, she pulled the thong off and walked over to my table, and she dropped them on my napkins and handkerchief. For the lights were nice and dim. She said the thought of you being in my presence right now makes me want to fuck you, she said tomorrow can't get here soon enough! She said TJ, you know what… call me later tonight. I said I sure would!!! Hey anything one would say to keep the peace, especially in public, Trish made it back to the table and we ordered, I had to grab the thong very smoothly and put them in my blazer because I at that time thought Trish seen them there lying on the handkerchief, but she didn't. The waitress had taken our order, and the thong was exposed before us all. Talking about a close call, I was shaken up, I think any man would've been at that time let's keep it all the way real, you aren't fooling me at all. After dinner we went to the movies, it was a popular movie that people had been waiting on since seeing the previews, anyway while standing in line for snacks, a couple was in front of us, they were arguing. It wasn't as if Trish and I were being nosy, I mean…. It went from one extreme to the next. The guy told the lady, you mad because I caught you cheating on me. He said I swear when we leave the movie theatre, I assure you I'm going to pack your shit and you're getting your sorry ass out of my house! He said we've been together all these years and you going to do some dirty shit like this…. Then y'all women have some fucking nerve to say, "why do men cheat"!! He said we cheat because no good ass women like you go sleeping around with best friends and shit! He said if you had received that phone call 20 minutes ago your movie ticket never would've been purchased, he said I tell you with everything I love I never would've paid for it! He said you mayest well call Brent and tell him…. I know about you two and tell him to pick you and all your shit up off the curb because that's where you all will be! He started making his way out of the theatre and she kept trying to say (let me explain!) How can you explain cheating is what many would say. The question should be, why my so-called friend though? Well, family and friends should be a no, no but sometimes they're the ones that'll fuck you! soon as you turn your head. A so-called friend, you can easily say I never have to see you again, but the family…. Now I'm sure that's going to hit differently. Then you have other family members trying to console you. saying things like blood is thicker than water, but then one should be able to understand when we say, "Why then"! You'll be surprised by the people that are trying to wear your shoes, some people want what you have so bad that you'll never know even your significant other they want it all. It's a dog-eat-dog world. Again, people tell on themselves if you have family and friends that say things like hook me up or introduce me to a lady like yours 10 times out of 10 he wants your lady this just so happens to be a fact. If they're hanging around, they're hanging around for a reason. So, it is important to keep your circle tight. Ask yourself "Why" are they always hanging around every Wednesday at the same time? And keep in mind fellas it's not always the man at fault, we must pay attention to our lady, although she may or may not have done a thing to lead one on, some people get signals crossed up because they've programmed their minds to believe that the person wants them and can be as wrong as running a red light you know or stealing from the church house. The shit that says your WRONG! That could also be a dangerous person so keep your eyes open, you might say Aww that's just how he or she is... yeah OK! If you can convince yourself of that, then who am I to say anything? But good luck to you I wish you nothing but the best. That was just a quick update now let's get back to the scheduled program. Follow me if you will. Trish said what do you think happened when they got outside? I guess she called that guy what... what his name Brent was it! Damn, she was dirty she wasn't thinking at all. You let me tell it she deserves what she gets I can't feel bad for her... well what do you think? Why You're so quiet? I was just listening sweetheart I respect your outlook on it, but do you believe he's been a squeaky-clean guy, I remember him saying for years they've been together. However, what is past tense is past tense. I'm glad you said that TJ, because you were beginning to scare me a bit! But yesterday doesn't have anything to do with today Trish said. Well, it all depends though! Trish said how you, figure? I said SHHHH-HHH we're in the theatre now... Trish said don't Sush me! I said Aww come on babe let's talk about this some other time, the movie will be starting soon. It's like why are you getting mad with me, that was between two people we don't even know! Trish said, I didn't like how you just shushed me and you're right we don't know them.... she said I'm just saying you seemed so insensitive! Trish, I don't know those people I don't care. Trish said I bet your ass would've cared if it was the lady hurting and torn! I said, Trish.... Please let's just drop that, because you are about to make a mountain out of a molehill. She said really! Oh, really TJ!! I remembered what my dad said when he said that he had been married to my mom for 50 years and he still doesn't understand her... Well, that was me at that time. I said you know what I don't care to watch this movie, let's go home. She grabbed her bag and took off walking down the steps from the theatre, I had to grab the bucket of popcorn and drinks so I could dispose of them as I made my exit. I heard someone say, what was their problem? It was that kind of night Y'all. Believe me, I was thinking the same thing whoever it was that said what was their problem.... The only one that had a problem was Trish. When I got to the car, I said Trish why are you letting your emotions get the better of you? I may as well have been talking to myself because Trish didn't say anything to me. I said OK that's what we are doing then, because if you don't want to talk to me surely, I can't make you. I love you anyway. Trish said yeah….. do yourself a favor and don't say anything else tonight to me! It's funny how we men have to take and put up with our lady attitude, even when we don't know why she is fussy or when she's fussy about things that don't concern us. Well, if I needed a reason to go cheat then that would've been a green light for me, I can't lie. I knew we had to get home and no matter how much I tried to forget about what happened with me and Lori honestly, I couldn't… and not to mention the thong drop a Lil' earlier, did I smell it yes. Did I call her "no"? I was surely thinking about it, I tell you no lies, but I ended up pouring myself a drink and fell asleep on the couch. I woke up to go take a leak around 0330 or so I stumbled to the bathroom and straight from there, I went and got in the bed. The very next morning I woke up to Trish riding me. I wasn't expecting that, especially with what happened last night, but hey, I guess that was her way of paying me back. After we were done, I said how about some breakfast, she looked at me and said only because I love you. I got out of bed took a shower got dressed and what do you know just in time for breakfast… Trish said TJ, your co-worker you introduced me to last night, I want to know why was she looking at me rolling her eyes she did it numerous times, you knew her before me or something, because no woman is going to do that rolling the eyes not unless something has been shared between two, or if I'm wearing something or should I say I was wearing something so good to a point to where she becomes envious. I said that's it, sweetheart!!! You looked so beautiful, especially last night babe! I saw a lot of guys that took a peek!! I went on to tell her you're beautiful from head to toe, that's why I made you mine. I said Trish remember when you said Lori was pretty, but not prettier than you? She said yes, I remember saying that what about it! I said Well one thing I can tell you about Lori, well from what I was told, she always has a competitive outlook so maybe she was looking at you for those reasons! Trish said but why would she call herself competing against me this makes no sense! I said maybe it's a woman thing…. You know how y'all are! Trish said that better be all… Because she doesn't want any problems with me! As I was making my way to sit at the table and eat, Trish thought I didn't hear when she said you don't want any problems either! I heard her. I intend to treat her right! I would like to think that's all of us men, but in hindsight, it's 2020. Do I speak for the world, well no I do not. but if I can be a voice I would rather it be a positive one. After I ate breakfast, we went to church and I tell you if it isn't one thing it's another, I couldn't believe my eyes, I saw my ex I hadn't seen in years…. well, you know it's one of those things when you broke up, but you can't remember why you broke up. That was me when I saw her. Before my eyes, there was one of my exes Deja. What I didn't know was she knew my lady, Trish, so after a nice morning of breakfast and giving my praise to The Creator, I said help me, because I knew problems were on the way!!! TJ this is my co-worker she just moved back to NC recently Deja, TJ… TJ Deja. I hesitated to see what Deja was going to say and she was as shocked as I was, we both played it off as if it was our first time meeting, but we know our history…. I just followed her lead. I admit she was looking good! I started thinking Damn what did I do to mess that up! So many thoughts were playing on my mind. I guess I understand when they say let's leave the past in the past yeah that works until your past is staring you in your face. Another fine job TJ, what more do you have for me…. Yeah, I recall saying something like that. Trish said Deja is so sweet, she went through a tough situation with her ex-husband. All I know is he's a sorry man for what he did to Deja and her children. I asked how many kids Deja had. Trish said she has 2 a girl and a boy, she said the boy's dad is somewhere in Raleigh, but the girl's dad is by her ex-husband who lives in Las Vegas. Wait Trish you said the boy's dad is somewhere here in Raleigh…. well, does the boy know him? Trish said Deja has an idea, but she's not sure, I guess it's embarrassing to her not knowing. Well, I know it would be for me! How many of you men, out there would be thinking the same thing I was thinking? Aww man he was my son, knowing you two had history, I was thinking Damn why Deja would not tell me back when if I was the father. Trish was talking and I promise words were coming out of her mouth, but I couldn't hear not one word she was saying, I was zoned out. Well to be honest I was sad for Deja because I know this woman and she doesn't deserve that, she was so sweet when we were together, now she may have changed after our relationship, I still just don't see it! I made my way back to my car while coming out of the grocery store remember when I said Trish was talking to me and I didn't hear any words coming out of her mouth, well Trish had invited Deja over for Sunday dinner. I know right oh well! To insult the situation a song sung by "Keith Sweat" and "Gerald Levert" comes on the radio the song was "Just One Of Them Things" Talk about timing well there you go R.I.P "Gerald Levert". Trish said there's nothing like old R&B back in the day, I agreed, but then I said to myself other than the sweet loving this morning add the breakfast and church she had my vote, but inviting Deja to Sunday dinner is way wrong I thought! Then I started thinking thoughts like maybe I was putting too much thought into the situation. Relax and stop being selfish, yeah that's what I said, but how much of that was I believing? Huh, not much at all I tried motivating myself you know, especially when I thought about what I was getting ready to face. We got home and I took the groceries in the house after stopping by the grocery store, we changed clothes I started flying my team colors you know that football team that plays on Sundays they wear Black and Gold yeah them that have 6 rings they're in western P.A. anyways, Trish started dinner I was maybe

45 minutes into the game next thing you know the doorbell rung…. Trish yelled from the kitchen Honey can you go get the door? As soon as I got up to go open the door my phone started ringing, I said who would be calling me now? I opened the door and Who's there Deja, I said come on in, I took her jacket and hung it up and I told her Trish was in the kitchen she said let me go and say hello. I said no problem she took a sticky note and an ink pen from her purse and started writing she handed me the sticky note with her phone number and address with a message that said we need to talk as soon as possible; I just nodded my head up and down letting her know ok cool! My phone started ringing again and it was Lori calling. As Deja made her way into the kitchen that sad feeling came over me again. I answered my phone Hello. How are you TJ, I hope you're feeling fine, because I would like for you to finish the Masterpiece today. I said hello Lori. I'm doing just fine I went on to tell her I'll be able to finish the Masterpiece today, I said to Lori after dinner and the conclusion of my game, I'll make my way over OK. Lori said why didn't you call me like you said you were, I said are you serious as if you didn't see me out on the town with my significant other last night and you know how naughty you were Miss Thong Dropper. Lori started laughing and she said did you smell the strawberries? I said I caught a whiff when I put them in my blazer pocket. Did it give you an erection baby, I said Lori let me get ready to eat so I can make my

way over, Lori said but answer my question before you hang up! I said yes it made my Carolina Wood get even harder, I whispered to her. Well TJ you know we're going to fuck up my bed sheets when you get here so be prepared! I hang up my phone, I hear my ex in the kitchen talking. While looking at the game I said to myself if she knew Deja was my ex, would she be in our home getting ready to have dinner with us? I don't think so, well if I can answer that then what is she going to do when she finds out? Is she going to quit her job, is she going to try to come see me with gloves? Some murder mystery if you will. I surely hope not, yeah that's what I kept telling myself. Trish said babe come eat, get washed up, and come eat. I said OK as my team was winning big it's late 3rd quarter and looks like we got this game baby I'm happy! I washed my hands and made my way to the dining room. We all sat down I blessed the food and the chicken parmesan oh my God was award-winning with the sweet corn on the cob with whatever seasoning she put on it and the Caesar Salad with that garlic bread it all satisfied my tastebud. I don't know why Trish thought it was a good idea to bring up what happened last night while we were out on the town. Trish said Deja, TJ introduced me to two of his co-workers last night while we were at dinner, and I looked up well every time I looked up to all eyes on me! Felt as if I was 2Pac or some shit! They stared me in the face rolling their eyes... I mean every time I looked up. Oh my God, I wanted to pop her so bad!!! Deja chimed in a bit and said…. She probably was a bit jealous. Trish said Well to her credit she was a pretty lady she's very pretty and had a nice body. But for her to kept looking at me the way she was it made me think she wasn't sure of herself. You know Deja that's the difference between us grown mature women and those young ladies trying to figure it out. Deja said I agree. She said but did you stop to think she may have the hots for TJ! Deja said the reason I said she may have the hots for TJ is because of me being a woman and being alert and I've had some similar situations a few times where the younger ladies were trying to get my husband's attention in public and look at what eventually happened with him and myself…. We're no more you know. Trish said that Bitch wishes she was me I mean even if she wants TJ, who is he with! Now I sympathize with you Deja. but there was just something about her that I just couldn't take, and besides TJ is smarter than that he chose right! I can't lie when I heard my lady say those things, I wanted to give her a supply of the Carolina Wood! Hey, the way she stood up for me I wanted her in a steamy, steamy way! I said damn that wine got my lady going in, She's on 10! But she was wearing it well! Deja said Well It's good to know you're a very confident woman Trish! Trish said I'm very confident and I'm not easily to be moved. You know what else Deja…. TJ is doing artwork at her house. Deja said WHAT!!! He's doing artwork at her house! Oh, wow ok now well maybe you need to look into that a bit more. Trish said I trust TJ, because I give him love every day show him love every day and share my pot of gold with him whenever he wants it or whenever I want to shine off. I mean they were talking as if I wasn't there! Deja said ooooo-k!! I admire your confidence, Trish. Look at you!! Deja said I was always empowered, but I'm very empowered after hearing another woman talk like that! I figured this was one of those women moments, I know Deja well, but was she empowered or was she playing with Trish? Hmmm, I wonder. Deja said, TJ so you're doing artwork for her are you? I said yes, I am. Deja said honestly do you think Lori likes you? I said of course or there's no way I would be in her home doing the job. Deja said Well let me say it in another term… DO you think Lori got the hots for you; you know like someone that wants to have SEX with you? I knew what she meant in the beginning, I was just being a smart-ass I knew what she was searching for! I responded no I don't think so, we have the same manager at work, and we all know the saying. It's not cool to get coochie where you get your paycheck… what's the other one the other saying that says Don't dip your pen in the company's ink, yeah all that stuff, but how many of us fail? Deja said I'm sure the number is staggering, but it surely doesn't stop a lot of you men from engaging now do it. I said absolutely not, I said let me explain something here… I mean it's damn if we do Damn if we don't. Take a wind chime for example the wind chime just hangs from a tree branch correct? Deja said yes, most time. I said without a swift breeze what good would the wind chime be? She said Well if it's decorative then it can be pretty to look at. I said correct but useless, I said you women are much like a wind chime at times, y'all can be still and sweet for a minute, but when we men give, or should I say, show attention the swift wind if you will you start Jingling and when a strong wind comes through, you're mute why.... because like you said. Maybe the number is staggering and there you are feeling some sort of way, but yet y'all want to put the ownness on us men as if we're wrong I mean sure you can wear whatever you want, but why get mad when the attention you're getting is unbearable well isn't that what you wanted, what are you looking to accomplish sweetheart! Was that not part of the way you got the man? Because people of the world can stop with all the lies, like when they say looks don't matter, well if that's the case, then be content with an old raggedy-ass car that barely starts. Ask yourself what happens "when" they can afford a new car... they get it end of story! Trish said Well I guess he told us didn't he Deja! Deja said I see why you say Damn if you do Damn if you don't. It makes total sense. She said Trish looks like you got yourself a keeper for now. Trish said that's my baby ohhh-hhh I love myself some TJ!!! Even if he makes me mad, I love him anyway, because there's always going to be someone who looks better and has a better body, but my quality is unmatched at that point it will all fall on TJ. I said keep going honey, I'm so in love with you right now! She smiled. Oh, it was such a beautiful smile! While eating my dessert that tasty Honey bun cake Deja looked at me and winked her eye. I said ladies I have to get going, I have work to do so Trish, I love you and Deja take care! As I was making my way through the living room the score had even worsened, I was happy with how my squad handled business. I made my way over to Lori's house to finish the artwork. Maybe, I think too much, because there I was thinking about how beautiful my lady Was and knowing what I was about to face in a few minutes. If you're not wearing my shoes, I'm not saying you're shoeless, it's just saying wear your own, Only The Creator can judge me. Ring the doorbell. I was greeted with a Hey TJ and a kiss on the cheek Lori was on a phone call so I just started getting her masterpiece done moving as fast and precise as possible yet making it a masterpiece. Lori has music playing, throughout the house, and a song by "Calvin Richardson" came on "Treat Her Right" This just so happens to be a nice song, and next thing you know Lori comes out wearing some sexy lingerie! I said oh my, my why me! I'm trying my best to look away and avoid the lust, Lori didn't have to try that hard.... because I was done when she walked up to me and nestled closely to me and put my hands on her booty. She said you like seeing me in this lace, do you? In a sexy voice. I said you look very alluring. She said do I excite you TJ? I said you do that for sure, but why are you doing that to me when you know I have a lady! Lori said you don't love her like you think you do. I said Well I think a bit differently, I do love my lady! She said if you loved your lady, you wouldn't have a hard-on. I said you can't be serious, I'm only human, I'm no robot! Lori said It's self-control and so you are telling me, I have control over you. I said easily you said that! But then why are you doing what you're doing or should I say does this still stem from your fantasy or fantasies? Lori said Well you'll be forever an ongoing fantasy TJ. I said nothing lasts forever Lori. Meanwhile, my phone started ringing and it was my buddy, Allen. I answered.

Hello.

Allen said what's up TJ, what you got going on right now? I said Man I'm just trying to finish some art. All the while there Lori was giving me a hand job, Allen said Man you alright. I said oh yeah, it's just this art chemicals, but what's up? Allen said I went to work and got some overtime and Brandi said she saw you with your lady last night, I said yeah, I did see her and Lori. Allen said yeah, I know and started laughing. I know you remember when I said if I didn't know any better, I would think you two have something going on! I said Allen what are you talking about? He said oh Brandi told me what happened I said Al let me call you back, he said no problem. I said Lori what's up with you why did you tell Brandi what happened between us? Lori said because that's my best friend. She's been my best friend, since college, and we share everything! But you're not in college anymore, so why couldn't you just "Hush" Lori said don't sit here and tell me that you won't going to tell Allen what happened between you and me I know y'all men talk! I said Well I wasn't truth be told... I guess we'll never know now will we, I mean Damn.... I give you a sample of the Carolina Wood and you want to go tell the world, because we all know Brandi tells everybody business! Lori said that's my friend I said Well you should've known better Lori! Lori bent over and took my Carolina Wood out and no matter how upset I was with her, there I was putting it to her. Well after we finished, she said that's who I was talking to when you got here. I said figures. Lori said Aww so I see you're upset about that; I gave you some fancy wet and you're still angry. I just displayed some awesome hip work and yet you're grouchy. I never thought you would be this angry behind that TJ. I said it's a small world Lori and, in our field, It's even smaller. Lori said Well look at it positively how about that? I said are we left with any other choice! I said Lori I got to finish up the masterpiece it's getting a little late and we have to work tomorrow, she said OK. Lori said TJ you're in trouble. I said why did you say that, Lori. She said I'm falling in love with you. I said how can you be falling in love with me so soon, maybe it's just the Carolina Wood you're in love with, I mean you haven't known me long enough to be in love with me. Lori said I understand I hurt you, because you just let your emotions show, and that's enough to make any woman's wheels turn from lust to love. Well at the point she just made, I couldn't argue that, so I responded I respect how you feel and all, but again sweetheart, Trish is my lady and that's just it. please understand I have no idea what the future holds for only The Creator knows. Maybe soon you'll get over me and I'll be a memory. Lori said Well is that how you are going to look at me? I said Lori, I'm left with no choice! Again, I got a lady at home. That's all I can say. Never did I lead you on, If I did then I'd feel somewhat guilty, but you chose me and you going to look at me as if I'm wrong, I even tried avoiding your plight. I mean no disrespect to you, you're a beautiful woman and could have any man in the world, but you just can't have me in the way you want, I'm sorry. Lori said please just don't trash me moving forward. I said I have no desire to do that Lori, we don't know what fate may bring. Lori said Well I guess we'll just have to wait and see huh? I said I guess so. I finished the masterpiece and we both celebrated, she gave me a check and she was so thrilled about the masterpiece! Another satisfied customer! I made it home and my lady said I missed you! I said Aww come on.... I was only gone a few hours honey. Trish said I know, but whenever you're not here it just doesn't seem the same. I get lonely. I said you see how you validate me. Trish said I don't understand! I said did you not just say you get lonely? Trish said I'm just saying...I cut her off and said "We" us "men" must work even odd hours to finance our lifestyle, you know sweetheart you women want the world, but you all cranky when the work comes calling, so what I'm saying is you can't have the lifestyle without some sacrificing. I'm afraid that's not how life works. Trish said Well hey man I was just missing you! I said I was missing you too, so I guess we're even. Trish started laughing and said God I love you so much TJ!!! I went to take a shower and when I got out Trish said come and get some of this pot of gold! I obliged! We were just passionate as if it was our 3rd or 4th time doing the naughty! After the lovemaking, I asked her about Deja. I said Trish how long did Deja hang around? She said maybe another hour after you left Trish said, what's funny is how she was talking like she knows you or something! I said Aww shit here we go!! I responded well why do you say that? Trish said because she knows your likes she even knew your favorite football team. I said Well she should, because I was only watching the game when she came in and she saw me in my Jersey. Trish said Damn I didn't even think about that, but when she said you seem to be a briefs guy because you wouldn't like to have your Wood flapping all over the place in some loose boxers, I said wow!!! That's exactly what you be saying! Because you do say that babe! I said Well maybe her ex-husband had similar thoughts you know. Trish said maybe, but it's only one of you. I said Damn right! And I started thinking yet again I said to myself, Deja is about to be a problem. I kissed my lady and told her I love you goodnight. I went on and prayed as I always do. Only this time I was praying that The Creator will keep the problems away. He always answered my prayers so there was no need for me to think any different

Goodnight.

Alarm sounding

6:45 am. Cole in my eyes the morning Carolina Wood is asking if there will be any action this morning. Not this morning my buddy. I do my usual routine and before leaving I check the mirror for validation, kiss my lady, and tell her to have a blessed day of course the mirror says validated. I got to work and there were so many stares as I made my way down the hall, I heard someone call me TJ! There's my buddy, Allen, he said Man I thought you were going to call me back! I said Al man, I got so much going on don't take it personally, but I was so busy. Al said TJ, I hope it was worth it. I responded Al you have no idea. I got to my workstation and on my desk, there was a rose on my desk, and I knew who this came from. Well, so I thought anyway! I noticed Lori walked by without saying good morning, Hmm that's strange, odd even. I knew some shit was on the way, so I opened my desk drawer and there was a note. I was looking around and I noticed all eyes were on me. The note reads from an admirer…. if you want to know who gave you the beautiful rose, I'll be in the breakroom sitting at the table near the vending machine. Meet me there at 9:15, Al said Damn TJ you got Lori buying you a rose…. He said you gave her a few acres of the Carolina Wood didn't you LOL! I said dude this didn't come from Lori!! Allen said Damn who else are you supplying around here! I said no one else! Al said SHIT! you lying to me!! I said naww bro I'm serious. Al said TJ heads up. Lori said you move fast, don't you!! I said hello, and good morning to you. Lori said yeah good morning, whatever! Who the hell is that rose is from!!! I said oh so it's not from you! Lori said so, after the talk we had yesterday you think I would turn right around and buy you a fucking rose? You are full of yourself dude. I said Well honestly, I have no idea who the mystery person is. Lori said yeah, yeah anyway and walked off. I know what this may look like to Lori especially after we came to an understanding if you want to call it that. But I truly have no idea who the rose came from! Al said what are you going to do TJ? I said I'm going to find out who bought me the rose that's what I going to do! Allen said I'm sure you going to find out, but good luck to you man. I smell the fragrance from the rose stem it smells familiar, but come on TJ me trying to find out by walking around trying to get a whiff of every woman wouldn't be the smartest move, and to be honest, whoever it maybe could be wearing the same fragrance as someone else…. Aww what the heck! I'll just wait till 9:15. Anticipation

I remember looking at my watch it was 9:08, I said close enough I took off out of the lab I de-gowned and I made my way to the breakroom. I walked in and I saw my supervisor sitting at the same table the note mentioned, although I was a Lil' early I started saying I know full well, my supervisor isn't the mystery lady… she wouldn't go there oh no I wouldn't think! But then again. Hmm…. My supervisor finished her coffee and looked up and saw me getting a drink from the vending machine it was now 9:13 something told me to stand down and I did. My supervisor said good morning, TJ, I said good morning, Divia how are you, Divia said Well it's Monday morning ask me when it's time to clock out. LOL! I said I know that's right, terrible weekend huh? Divia said it's just that they go by so fast. I said that they do. It's 9:15, Divia said are you behaving yourself TJ? I said of course I always do my best. She gathered her belongings and said have a good day today. I said you have yourself a wonderful day as well. It's now 9:18 I had my mind made up. I said this got Lori written all over it! As I was getting ready to exit the break room, in came Amber. Amber said hello TJ how are you on this Monday morning and went on to say…. I hope you had a nice weekend! I said good morning to you as well Amber, I said I had a nice weekend thank you. I said Well Amber I must go back to work. Amber said TJ come talk to me for a few after she prepared her coffee, she sat in the same seat that the note stated, and I said oh shit!!! You're the mystery lady who bought me the rose? Amber said it was me, I'm the mysterious woman. Sure enough, I smelled that fragrance from off the rose stem and note. I complimented her smelling so sweet and nice. I said thanks for the rose as well, but it's not my Birthday, or Christmas, or anything for one to be so sweet surely it isn't Valentine's Day, what do I owe to this? Amber said sorry I wasn't in here seated at 9:15, but some issues came up you know how it goes in the labs, I said oh that I do. I made my way up here to the breakroom at 9:08 and when I came in Divia was sitting at the same very table you said you'd be sitting at. Amber said no-ooo-oo! I said yes! Amber said did you mention anything about the rose? I said no, I was just following her lead. Amber responded you're a smart man, but I didn't know how to get you to notice me so I decided the rose would do it! I was the first one here other than the security guard, so no one saw me. I said wow so let me ask you something. Was this something you planned? Amber said TJ we women plan everything, yes even us white women! I believe you all have that in common all the women around the world. I would like to talk more but I must get back to work. Amber said here's my number and she went on to say you may want to hear what I want to talk to you about. I said I'll reach out the first chance I get. Thanks for the rose again! She said I'll be seeing more of you; I'm thinking to myself again y'all! Let me explain something here to you all about Amber... Although she's not an Ebony

Queen or Latin Spice she can rival any of them for sure, I'm telling you all theirs so many women at my employer… well excuse me but at our employer, the women here turn their nose up when Amber come through the doors, they give her all kind of salty and hateful looks. I can relate because here I am a handsome Black man, but mostly the hate comes from the people who share the same color as me. Sickening I tell you. They smile in your face and yet they want to gut you like a fish. Somebody out there knows what I'm talking about If not maybe they're the individuals that's holding the knife. To all you non-haters watch yourselves out there, your boy may not be your boy as I mentioned in the entry keep your circle tight and don't trust them any further than you can throw them. You can tell the one that leaks hate just watch how they act towards you. Again, be careful. Allen said who is the mystery woman you been gone long enough! I said Well I can't say anything right now, I'll say this much though Divia was sitting at that very table that the note read. Allen said I know you were like no way! I said exactly. I said Al man it's hard to be monogamous. I mean it's like you know you got a good thing at home, and you know your lady feels the same way about you. Al said I hear you man, He said but how much of that do we bring on ourselves? I said I hear you there, but what about when it's not you that brings these things on yourself. Al said I don't know what to tell you TJ. I'm sure you'll figure it out. Al said Lori came over to see if you were back, she was pissed when she saw you weren't at your desk, I said oh yeah. Allen said expressions don't lie, and the look on her face seemed as if she had some choice words for you! I said I'll hear about it before the day ends, I'm sure. I owe this woman nothing though you know what I'm saying! Al said TJ, I wish I could help you, but then again no, no I'm good you'll figure it out.

Meanwhile

Deja, I do question TJ about wedding dates…. He put it all on me, he told me to come to him when I pick a date. Deja said oh so the ball is in your court. You two have been engaged for two years and no wedding date yet. That would scare me if it was me truth be told. Think about it Trish I mean what kind of game is he playing if he can't help you with picking the date for y'all wedding? If I were you, I'll be grilling his ass about a damn date! Trish said you know you got to sometimes go put fire under his feet is what you're saying!! You want to marry him right… because you make me think your content, Trish! I mean if you are fine with just being his lady his girl or his arm candy, then don't let me bother you with what I'm saying, forget what Deja has to say! Trish said you know what…. I'm going to talk to his ass later today. Thank you, Deja it's time for his ass to man up with helping me with our wedding planning. Hell, if it will even be one now! This makes me angry now when I sit here and think about it, here we all are getting older, and we're carrying on as if we're 23 or some shit! Meanwhile, Who is the rose bitch! I'm sure you have found out by now, you were gone for 47 minutes! Lori, I'm not even going to go there, and besides she doesn't work in here in this lab. Lori said you must think I'm fucking stupid! Calm down Lori, there's no need to act all crazy now! OH SO NOW I'M CRAZY TJ!! Lori, you're being too loud. I thought we had an understanding. Well, what do you want me to do? Lori, I didn't ask for any problem and you're making a scene. Lori said LIKE I GIVE A DAMN!! I told you yesterday how I was falling in love with you, but you want to FUCKING PLAY ON ME, and now throw me away as if I'm trash and I'm nobody's trash not even yours!!! Hey TJ, you got a minute can you come help me with something right quick it would only take a second excuse me honey, Can I borrow TJ just a second PLEASE... I promise he can come right back! WAIT JUST A MINUTE BITCH!!! I know you didn't just.... Hello Brandi Hi TJ. COME ON LORI!! Let's not go to that level, we have a career here come on Lori let's not lose it all behind a man that's not yours. I'll hurt that BITCH!!! SHE doesn't know me, Brandi!!! I went to help Amber and it was only a second, she had no idea what was going on, on our side of the hall. I knew for sure I was in deep trouble. I felt bad for Lori because truly I didn't think she was really in love with me like that. I mean she threw a punch at Amber and if Amber would've seen her throw a punch at her I don't know what would've happened! Thanks to The Creator Amber had her back turned heading back across the hall and thanks to Brandi although I know Amber heard Lori as loud as she was, even my boy Allen was trying to defuse the heated moment! I of course heard the haters talking to Brandi and Lori trying to brainwash Lori spewing hate and envy I guess they were preying on Lori's vulnerability; I laugh at them. A Pitiful bunch for sure. Allen said TJ, my guy your up shits creek without a paddle. I'm going to pray for you brother! I mean Damn Lori threw a punch at Amber!! But why Amber, what does she have to do with anything, she works across the hall. Wait a minute, TJ she's the mystery rose lady? I said yes sir. My boy Allen just stood there with his mouth open! TJ how long have you and Amber been hooking up man you're a bad mothafucka!!! But does Lori know Amber is the mystery lady? I said that's what I don't know! But I thought I heard Lori say I know you're the Bitch that bought that rose. Allen said Lori was talking so much shit…. She probably did say that! I surely don't doubt it. Amber entered the lab again…. TJ, I need you one more time I'm sorry Allen. IS THAT BITCH OVER HERE AGAIN!!! Allen said chill out Lori come on now you're better than that. Lori said SHUT THE FUCK UP ALLEN! Amber said wait a minute is she talking to me? I said no… I don't think so! Let's not keep the work waiting! Amber said she was in a rage when I needed your help earlier, is she your lady or something TJ? I responded no she's not my lady, I try to be cool with

everybody, but I'm in a shit storm all of a sudden with her…
Amber said but why? I said I would have to tell you some
other time. I helped Amber again and made my way back to
my station, Allen said heads up TJ, but Divia called me and
asked what's the situation in the lab. I said seriously! Allen
said someone went and said we had major problems here in
the lab, I responded should I wonder who.…I mean there are
quite a few of us that work back here so who knows. But I
do have an idea who the culprits are. Surely this makes the
haters happy. I wonder who went and told? Allen said I'm
sure Divia going to want to talk to you, but it's probably going
to be in your favor! I said we'll see. I started reading foul
messages Lori put on my Desk. I asked Al if he knew anything
about them, and he said he was in the office being interviewed
about the Lil' incident in the lab. I know he was telling me
the truth, he's like my Lil' brother. Well …. Sure enough, I
was called to the office and Divia said I just asked you this
morning were you behaving yourself did I not? I said yes you
did. Divia said what's the problem… what's going on back
in the labs? I said honestly, it's a personal thing but, if I must
say a certain young lady is having issues with me rejecting
what she wants, really it's that simple. Divia said TJ come on
man, not on the job you know things can get messy when
working with someone and you're trying to date! I said I'm
afraid you don't understand. I said again I rejected her
advances towards me. Divia said Well why is she starting

problems if you saying you aren't interested? I said that's what I'm trying to figure out myself, can I be totally honest with you Divia! Divia said, of course, let's hear it. I said it started with Lori asking me to do a piece of art for her, for which I asked what kind of art piece and she said, she wanted me to draw a masterpiece of herself. Divia said Well there's nothing wrong with that, I want a picture of myself done in a nice medium of my choice! I responded she wanted me to do a masterpiece of her in the nude. Divia said ohhh-hh K wow! I said I agreed to do the art for which she requested, but Divia… Lori was looking for more. Divia said what TJ? What more could she have wanted? I said she came unto me sexually I regret I obliged! Divia said OK now I see, she said how long have you two been seeing each other? I just did the artwork last Friday and I finished the piece Sunday yesterday. Divia said so this is very fresh, how can she be head over hills that fast. I just looked like well hey…. and went on to say she saw me and my significant other out to dinner Saturday and I even introduced my lady to her. Divia said wow TJ man. I said I know; I know. Divia said I'm going to let you take the rest of the week off, but one last thing what role did Amber play in this, I said she simply walked to our lab and asked me for assistance. Really that's all? I said that's all Divia. This by the way TJ isn't a write-up, I'm just giving you some time to clear your head a bit. I said thank you. From the looks of it, I would've thought Divia was mesmerized. Hey, you never know. I went back to the lab and cleaned my desk and workstation, Allen said what's up TJ! They didn't fire you, did they? I said no sir they just gave me the rest of the week off. Al said with pay because shit!!! I need to have a situation to pop off, but I am not you they may fire my ass! LOL, I told Allen I'll call him later. I was making my way out of the lab and Brandi said TJ why did you hurt my friend like that? Brandi, your friend hurt herself, I was totally up front with her, and she knew I was upfront with her. Brandi said, but she's spinning it a bit differently. I responded well you should know your friend, but do you believe your friend? For I have no reason to lie. I mean you saw her actions at the restaurant Saturday night, who plays with herself and then does a thong drop on the table or did you not see that or did you go blind all of a sudden, let's be real and honest here now. Brandi said TJ did you not see how fast Lori fell in love with you so quickly! Well Brandi that's all on her... How can that be my fault? Brandi said, well I hope you're happy Lori is suspended!! I'm sure you got your head really in the air now with that white she Devil across the hall! I walked off and said have yourself a good rest of the day Brandi. You know it's funny how people try to make you look bad or even guilty when things don't work out the way they wanted it to go. It's dangerous when you think about it. I left my employer, and I went to the grocery store on my way home, I'm picking up items to make myself a lasagna for dinner tonight. While shopping I hear voices on the next aisle, but I heard them talking saying things like Damn somebody is wearing a good-smelling cologne. I heard a voice say if he looks like that cologne smell he's in some trouble! I laughed and made my way to check out my items. Pay it forward if you will. Never thinking about what was about to happen. I heard excuse me maybe two or three times turning around on the fourth excuse me. One of the ladies said Damn! I said hello, as the grocery line was slowly moving. One of the ladies said I like that cologne you have on, what's the name of that fragrance you're wearing? I responded I have so many fragrances, but I told her I think it's the original Dolce & Gabbana. She says Damn that smell so good and she said I can't lie I even told my girlfriends if you look like that cologne smell, then you'll be in some trouble I responded oh noooo-ooo I surely don't want any trouble Lord no! She introduced herself, I'm Stacey then her other friends introduced themselves Abella and Coi. I said nice to meet you all, I'm TJ. I told them I was on the very next aisle when you made that comment about my cologne and now, I'm going to be in trouble if I ... Stacey cut me off and said oh my God you heard that!!! I surely did I went on to say I see you ladies dressed for the gym very nice I must say. Coi said thanks and yes that's where we're headed. I said I'm just getting off work myself and here I am picking up some items to prepare a lasagna for dinner. I then hit the gym after dinner around 6, or 6:30. Stacey said Well are you… Abella cut her off and said talking to 3 women doesn't bother you! I said not at all, should I be? Coi cut Stacey off and said you never know. I said true, but you all seem to be some nice ladies. Stacey said don't cut me off anymore… neither one of you!! She said TJ it seems as if I've seen you. I said maybe a time or two, I'm sorry I can't say the same. She said maybe it was the gym… Do you work out at Max Out Fitness? yes, I do, but I go to the one across town, not the one next door. The cashier rang up my items, I paid it forward and I said you all take care then I heard…. TJ I'm going to give you my number maybe you can help me with my workout at the gym then Coi and Abella said yeah maybe you can help us too. They all gave me business cards. I told the ladies well I'm not a trainer, but I will surely help you all in any way I can! You all have a great workout. I took my ass home thinking to myself again. I'm like what's going on TJ that's 3 beautiful women that gave you their numbers…. Don't you throw those cards out the window, I was so close to throwing the numbers out as I was driving home, I was trying to convince myself they only want help in the gym what harm is that? But they look nice though very sexy! I also noticed not one of those ladies wearing any rings on their finger, you will learn one-day TJ. I get home and I see Trish is home already, I said I hope she's alright. If she with the attitude, I have no problem going to my place. Got the groceries out and made my way into the house. I yell out Trish I'm home!

Trish said what are you doing here so early you're two and a half hours early. I told her I wasn't feeling good, and I just needed some time to myself.... I went on telling her, I took off the rest of the week as well. Trish said NEGRO are you saying you're FIRED!!! I said no just like I said I took off the rest of the week. Trish said TJ CUT THE SHIT! It's Monday... I mean how bad was your morning then.... Because taking off the rest of the week, just doesn't make sense to me. IS IT SOMETHING YOU'RE NOT TELLING ME? I just told you! I just don't feel good, and I need some time to myself! What more do you want me to say, I have no more to add than what I just said Damn! Trish said HOLD ON WAIT, DON'T get loud with me, because we need to talk NOT NOW, BUT RIGHT NOW!! I don't know what's going on over at your employer, but what you not gone do is take it out on me.... I'm not your fucking problem buddy!!! If I had wings, I would fly away is what I said to myself. I tell you again God understands us men, because in Proverbs 25:24 it read. Better to live on a corner of the roof than share a house with a quarrelsome wife. Although me and Trish aren't married surely, we're headed that way, hey don't get mad at me with what the word read! I dare you get mad at God. TJ are you listening!! You have my attention Trish go ahead. Well, I was talking to Deja today and she made me think about something. Just when I thought my day couldn't get any worse. "Here we go" Well kind of like our fight song we sing while cheering for my favorite football team that wears that Black and Gold. Those of you who know, know what I'm talking about. What did Deja have to say, Trish? Well, when I thought about it. I said is he playing games with me about getting married, I mean how long do you think we are supposed to be engaged? I FEEL SO FUCKING STUPID, 2 years and then you put it all on me about coming up with the wedding plans! Well, isn't that what you ladies do Trish? Y'all take our money and tell us to get out of the way!! You know it's confusing with you ladies' shit I said this, Sunday "Damn If We Do", "Damn If We Don't", but I guess that fell on deaf ears as well when I told you to come up with the wedding date and that I'll support it, or we'll come up with another date do you not remember! And how long ago was that TJ!! I hope you're not looking at me as I no longer have any value now that I've given you all of me even sexually, she said I'LL BE DAMN IF YOU GONE LOOK DOWN YOUR NOSE ON ME MOTHERFUCKER! I responded did it even occur to you that some people don't like to see when two people are happy in their relationship, so are you telling me that you're not happy? TJ how dare you disrespect Deja like that, you don't know her she's looking out for me because some ASSHOLE Ex husband of hers broke her and I'll be DAMN if it happens to me! Who do you live your life for Trish… hurt people hurt people do you not see that! My only beliefs are you women only know how you want your orgasm and sometimes you don't even know that! I guess that's why some of you say I can do it better myself and that's a lie.... When you ladies need a lifetime supply of Carolina Wood not rubber made or shit y'all put in your vaginas and who are you fantasizing about while doing you! X and Y chromosomes brought us here your mom and your dad fucking or making love or whatever it was they called it, just like my parents and everyone else parents that's facts! You need to apologize for wasting my time TJ, I'll do no such thing! Well, you need to leave and go to your place. I'm glad I have a place I can still call my own. As I walked out, I forgot something, so I rang the doorbell. Trish opened the door I walked back into the kitchen and grabbed my groceries. You may call it petty; I call it, I paid for it, and it will be my dinner! Some of you want everything even the things that don't belong to you. Get on my DAMN nerves!!! But we men are your problem. Huh, I laugh!

Why do men cheat huh?

I was so close to moving out well moving all my belongings to Trish's place a year ago, I had put my place up for sale, but I never got a buyer well I did, but the person ended up moving to Charlotte. It worked out for the best so welcome home TJ! Damn, this feels good this quiet peace of mind, I truly needed this. I'm disturbed by a phone call

Hello

Whoever it was they hung up. I figured it was Lori being mean. Now curiosity kills the cat, right we all heard that saying right? I said I was going to call and ask Deja what's with her influencing Trish although I have an idea, a good idea should I say. I know she's up to something. Come to think of it Trish has the nerve to tell me I need to apologize yeah right… when pigs fly and a cow oinks! You know what… I'm not cooking dinner; I'm going to just order some delivery. I'm really in no mood for pots and pans. I'll pour myself a drink though and again relax, this feels so awesome and I don't even have to get up and take my ass to work tomorrow, or the rest of the week either! You know what let me call Amber. Hello, this is Amber. Hi there this is TJ. Hi TJ, I'm glad you decided to call how's it going? I responded it's going, I guess one can say. Amber, how are you? I'm fine but a bit confused. Why are you confused what's up? Well, to be honest when I got off to work today, I stopped to get gas and the lady you were talking to this morning pulled in behind me while pumping my gas she was at the pump on the opposite side of me, I think I was on 3 and she was on 4. Anyway, she said let me tell you something stay away from TJ this will be the only time I tell you this! I said excuse me! Amber said if you said excuse me then you heard me. Wow, she said that! Do you have a few minutes to come out? I said sure meet me at Barnes & Nobbles at the mall, I'll be there in 45 minutes. We met, sat down, and started talking. Amber said I made sure to hurry and get here because of my being late this morning. I said no problem it was work-related you good! She said thank you. Amber said TJ, I've come across many scorn women, but I don't put anything past her. Here I am talking to you anyway. Some nerve I got huh! I admire your bravery. Thank you, Amber, said. She went on to say but she does have me a little paranoid. Hey, you'll be just fine no worries I responded. TJ what on God's green earth did you do to her for her turn so angry… I mean we cross each other at work she was always sweet to me the other lady I see her with all the time, but she's not so nice to me. But I would speak and keep on my way. I said Amber she hired me to do some art for her. Speaking of your art, I like the Mural you did for Michelle's son's room that's good work I must say! Thank you, Amber! Sure Ok, so she hires you…Well, she wanted me to do a masterpiece of her in the nude, I can't lie I wasn't going to do it, but I saw how badly she wanted it and I said I'll do it what the heck! Amber said I think that's every woman's fantasy. I said what fantasy is that. Amber said to have a man do a nice piece of art of us women in the nude especially a handsome artist such as yourself! Damn, I envy her for that one move! So last Friday night there we were one thing started and then another, I thought she would be able to handle it, but boy was I wrong. So, what happened

TJ…. You fucked her didn't you oh my God! We went there a few times, but believe me when I tell you, me having sex with her wasn't in my thoughts I tell you no lies. She came on strong and I couldn't resist. I'm only human. But now I blame myself for even doing well for accepting to do the job. Aww TJ baby when you fuck us good expect some problems Damn…. I'm scared of you woo-ooo-ooo baby let's get out of here! I have one more day of work then my vacation starts! I said oh wow vacation huh! I'm on a mini vacation for the rest of the week myself. Amber said are you serious? I said yes seriously! Amber said Well actually we can hang a little longer then! Do you care to come over to my place for a few drinks? I said please lead the way if you will.

Meanwhile

I told his ass he needs to leave because he hurt my feelings! Deja, you know TJ got too comfortable in our relationship, and all the while he never had intentions to marry me the negro just wasted my time! I feel so bad for you Trish I mean look at it this way you're a pretty woman that have so many beautiful outlooks, I mean you're the head of quality at one of the top pharma companies. And you and I both know that Charles like you. You'll be just fine and so you kicked TJ out, he's probably thinking Damn what was I thinking sitting in his lonely house right now. Huh, I don't think so!!! AWW TJ DON'T STOP…. DON'T STOP KEEP GETTING THIS PUSSY AWW YOU GETTING THIS CAKE GET

IT…. GET IT DON'T STOP HONEY I'M CUMMING ACAIN OH MY GOD YOU'RE THE BEST IT'S YOURS BABY IT'S YOURS WHENEVER YOU WANT IT, BABY!!! Damn TJ what did we just do… I can see how she lost her mind behind your ass and this was our first time… but I can tell you, it surely won't be the last that's for damn sure!!! I'm letting it be known right now so no surprise honey! You got me, I mean what more can I say speechless I am. You asked for it, I simply gave you what you wanted if I done fucked your head up don't blame me Lol! Fuck all this pillow talking I want you again TJ! Amber is a person who is upfront, she seems to know what she wants when she wants it. After we were done finally after the 4th time, I washed up and took it on in. I got home and said my prayers and off to sleep I went.

Alarm Ringing

6:35 a.m. I forgot to cut my alarm off for the rest of the week. Damn, alarm! Heck, I went back to sleep and woke up around 10:30. Thank you to The Creator for allowing me to see another day. I need to go to the grocery store I don't have any food, well no more than just the items I bought yesterday, those subs that me and Amber ate were good last night, I have no idea what market she purchased that meat from, it was so fresh. I looked at my phone, I saw that I had 20 missed calls. Damn bill collectors who I thought it was. what I was thinking, well I was wrong. I don't care for texting unless it's an emergency, why because some people play games with the messages. You may send one good or bad text and the immature adult you sent it to thinks it's a good idea to expose the message to the world. So, I let it be known if you want to talk to me talk to me over the phone line fuck a text. I guess it can be a gift and a curse though. But I prefer one to call. Hey, I'm old-fashioned, I'm cool with that. One thing for sure I'm no coward, I have no problem telling you face to face or over the phone line what's on my heart and mind. I tell you all what… Tell your mate from now on to call you over the phone lines not unless you're in public like the library or you're at work in a crowded breakroom or you're attending a ceremony or a concert or something I get why one would text then. How many relationships have sunk behind a text, the number may surprise us all, but then you may say how many relationships were saved by a text at the end of the day just know your mate. Again, I say it's a gift or curse. Do what works for you if it isn't broken don't fix it. May The Creator bless all of you that's in relationships and you're happy it's a beautiful thing I tell you! How's your day going Amber? It's going pretty well. I slept so well last night; I needed that last night TJ! I mean it's like, you knew my body so well that's impressive!! THANK YOU!!! I've been thinking about you all morning dude DAMN! I want you now sir! I can't lie I have been thinking about you too, I enjoyed you for sure you made a brother work for real you satisfied the Carolina Wood I must say! WHAT! I SATISFIED THE…. WHAT TJ? My package I call it The Carolina Wood. Amber said you do, do you! Well, I tell you what tell Carolina Wood to get ready for a good time later. I'm creaming right now as we speak TJ, I got to make you mines can we give it a try if things don't work out with you and your significant other? It's a possibility we'll see. TJ, I responded yes. I'm going to make it difficult for you to get back with her and trust me…. I have more to offer other than sex! I responded I'm sure you do! Amber said I dare you to try me. I said you never know. I heard a knock on my door, and I went to see who it was, I knew Trish was at work, and who else knows where I lived other than family and a few friends? Really though…. She can't be serious! Surprise TJ! Oh my God, I have been looking to finally have a moment with you. You're a dangerous person Deja! I would've thought you forgot my address. Thanks for tearing me and Trish apart. You're welcome, Deja said. Are you serious Deja!!! You shouldn't have done that…. That's wrong! Why didn't you mind your own business what made you think that was a good idea? TJ, you don't love Trish if you did then you two would be Mr. & Mrs. Right now, and you know I know you very well! Deja, yesterday is gone, and what's that supposed to mean she said? It means you don't know me today that's what it means! What you did was wrong! Trish told me you moved on from your husband. Deja said Well he left me for a 25-year-old. I thought it would be forever with him and he ripped my heart out TJ! I'm sorry to hear that, would you like something to drink, I do have wine and bottled water, but I haven't been to the grocery store. WHY ARE YOU INSENSITIVE TO ME TJ WHAT DID I EVER DO TO YOU? Don't cry, Deja. I hate that happened to you, I truly mean that now it's time for you to lick your wounds you know. Things surely will get better for you. It's easy to say but it's so hard to do TJ, I'm trying. I'm sure it's hard I can't say I understand, because I've never had a lady to wear my last name. Deja said it's because you're scared of that commitment. I have a question, Deja. Trish said you trying to find your son, Father, do you know who he is if you don't mind me asking? Deja said I don't mind you asking. YOU'RE THE FATHER! I just didn't want to tell you! WELL, aren't you going to say something? Ok, so you think I am supposed to jump for joy or something? How dare you, Deja!! What's wrong with you? So…. I have a problem OH BLAME DEJA WHY DON'T YOU! AS IF IT WASN'T YOUR FAULT I LEFT YOUR ASS…I got so sick and tired of the knocks on your door the sneaky phone conversations, you even had your brothers lie for you… your parents gave me warnings, but I loved you with all of my heart, you couldn't do any wrong and it eventually got the best of me and so I left your ass!! So, there you go BLAME ME…. BECAUSE I GREW TIRED OF YOUR SHIT!!! AND YOU THINK I'M GOING TO STAND HERE AND ENDURE YOUR SELFISH WAYS AS IF THIS IS PART 2, WELL I'M NOT

THE SAME EASY-GOING LADY IT'S A NEW DAY TJ!
I'm sorry I hurt you Deja, but why did you run? You know
you could've talked to me; you know that. I'm not being
insensitive to you Deja, but the past is where it belongs. We
must get through the day and anticipate a better tomorrow.
Stop crying I'm willing to do what I must do to make it right
how old is my son and where is he now? He's at his grandparent's
house his sister is as well. He's 7 years old. He's extremely
talented TJ. He's my boy of course he is! Awe I can't wait to
meet him I'm excited. I'm so-ooo-oo-ooo excited!! Dad is
here son! And by the way, your mother kept you from me all
your 7 years son! Deja, what are you doing you know....
Aww... you know what you're doing... Aww baby! You still
know how to make the tree stand tall! Follow me baby I'm
going to take of you. I'm going to make you feel really good!
For I know you want the Carolina Wood.... I saw that look
you had on your face when you saw me at that Church! That
look that said I know he still knows how to make that water
flow and come down. Tell me those were your thoughts! SAY
IT... SAY IT! YES, Those were my thoughts TJ Yes
Shhhhhhit....TJ!!!! I know how this may look to some of you.
You may be saying, Damn he was just having sex some few
hours ago. True indeed I would agree. I didn't ask.... for the
ladies who applied for the position. They were qualified so I
gave them the job. No need for name-calling at the end of
the day I'm a man. You know it's funny to hear people say

what they would and wouldn't do. If they were faced with that particular thing only then you're qualified. It irritates me when I hear that kind of talk, do me a favor and shut up! I sometimes hear talk like if he cheated once he'll surely cheat again, and the person that said that to you fantasized about a man that just caught her eye or a lady that caught his.... but yet she says she "only" has eyes for her significant other well if you're buying that, buy it for me too. This makes you a fool twice! I can give you 5 pennies and tell you to go and buy me a Ferrari and off you will go. SMH.... Meanwhile, Lori you need to turn the page with TJ, I mean the man Dick can't have you this far gone. I mean you're suspended from your job. He got your mind gone why are you giving him so much power over you Lori? Brandi, I don't want to hear the shit you're talking about... you can't tell me how I should or shouldn't be feeling these are my feelings, NOT YOURS! WAIT A MINUTE DON'T LOUD TALK ME!! I'm just concerned about my friend. Look at what he doing to our friendship! What is he doing Brandi? He's damaging our friendship! How's TJ damaging our friendship, Brandi? Have I changed towards you? Yes, you have Lori, we have known each other for years, I mean we go back way back since High School. So just because I want to be left alone or I'm not doing what you want me to do this is all TJ doing huh? Ugh yeah mmm-hmm! Well, maybe you are giving power to TJ. Ok, so you see that's the shit I'm talking about Pitiful! Look

Brandi Leave Me the Hell Alone!!! It's not just about his Dick, but how he treated me, He made me feel so special. He made me feel more special in 2 days than Teddy did in 3 and a half years! So, if this was never you. Please leave me alone! I suggest you go and find yourself a duplicate. Please let me reminisce, let me have my 2-day memory and I promise you'll never lose me as a friend. Brandi thanks for being concerned, but I'll be fine. Well, if you say so, I'll call you later. Just know if I don't answer I'm fine. I hear you Lori, I'm going to pray for you! Pray for your Damn self-Brandi! Thank you for hanging out with me Charles. Anytime Trish! I been waiting and anticipating this for years. Anticipating huh! So, you felt that this day would come Charles? I see you have confidence when you talk, that's a nice quality for a man! So, your man, wasn't confident is that what you're saying to me, Trish? Lord no. TJ invented the word confident. No disrespect but, it sounds like he was too confident, and yes, I knew this day would eventually come. But Deja mentioned you to me the other day. Hold on a minute! You say what? Say that again! Say what again Trish? You mentioned Deja did you not? Yes, she just thought it would be good if I came and talked to you and I'm so happy I listened to her! Wait a minute wait a minute let me figure this out!! Are you ok Trish is everything ok…. if I said anything wrong my apologies. I believe in taking things slow, but if you give me the green light, I'll take you wherever you want to go. Hey Trish, how are you, I looked up and said Bro isn't that Trish walking with another man! Because this motherfucka sure isn't our brother TJ. What's up with that Trish… Hello RJ well I don't owe you an explanation, but me and y'all brother took a break from each other. Excuse me fellas, but the lady has spoken! MAN, YOU BETTER SHUT THE FUCK UP!!! Before you find yourself getting up off the ground you've been warned! Hold on bro, I'm calling TJ now! Phone Ringing. Damn no answer, HEY Y'ALL SMILE! This picture doesn't lie. I'm surely going to send this to TJ! You were thinking with that one MJ! No doubt…. I'm all over this foul-ass shit bro. Trish who are these two guys? They're TJ brothers. Oh shit! Ok, but you did say y'all are taking a break, right? Because I can see how this may look to them. I don't have to repeat myself! Thanks for hanging out with me, but I need to go home. Well, let me walk you to your car! No, I'm fine Charles have a good night. Come on fellas we're good, right? MAN GET YOUR ASS OUT OF HERE! Do you think Trish lying MJ? Well, she always has been an honest person you let TJ tell it, but I believe her. I think she is lying! That's how a lot of us men end up getting hurt or killed. Behind a woman, then they'll go and lie on us as if they're the victim. Yeah, it's kind of like throwing the rock and busting the window, then hiding your hand like they didn't have anything to do with that window being busted, but you know RJ, that's the world we're living in today. Exactly RJ. So, Deja what's my son's name? His name is Teo. I like, I like, you know this don't just excuse you from leaving. You left without saying anything, so I gave you a couple of days to yourself and I remember trying to reach out to you, I called numerous times but your phone was cut off, so I stopped by your parent's house and your dad didn't tell me anything about you moving to Las Vegas. Your mom and your dad were looking at me with an angry face! I wasn't getting anything out of your parents and you know, I'm not a social media person, but for you and being concerned about you, I started a social media page, I saw some of your friends, but I never saw anything about you being abducted or anything bad, after checking back and forth, trying to find you, I became exhausted and finally after a year or so, I said I must move on. She'll come around sometime or another. Hey, what do you want me to do? Aww, I wouldn't have thought you cared. Honestly, I thought I was doing you a favor TJ. Oh, really Deja! So, this is like a game to you huh? I mean you may have thought I was deaf, dumb, and ditto but I planned the action, I just didn't know I had gotten pregnant. If I knew I was pregnant I probably would not have left like that... I still may have left though! Because I just couldn't put up with any more of your doggish ways. I remember seeing your friend Alyssa and she said, she hadn't heard anything from you. Ha... we talked every day! I told everyone if they see you to say that. I didn't find the humor in what you did DEJA! And you laugh as if it's funny!

"IMMATURE ADULTS", I TELL YOU… OH, I GET IT MONEY PROBLEMS CAME ABOUT HUH…. WELL, YOU CAN'T SPELL "DEBT" WITHOUT "EBT"!!! I KNOW YOU DIDN'T SAY I'M AN "IMMATURE ADULT", YOU OF ALL THE ADULTS IN THE WORLD! NO, WHAT'S NOT FUNNY IS WHEN THE WHOLE TOWN IS LAUGHING AT YOU, THAT'S NOT FUNNY!!!! AND BY THE WAY FUCK YOU AND THAT "DEBT"…. "EBT" SHIT YOU TALKING ABOUT! THE EMBARRASMENT I ENDURED…. SO DON'T SIT HERE AND TELL ME ABOUT HUMOR HUH THE NERVE OF YOU MR.!! Ok so again that was in the past Deja, I don't need a reminder, I've apologized for my foul actions, please don't keep throwing gasoline on flames that are calming down. Again, I stand accused. But you don't get a person back by running away and coming back bright-eyed and bushy-tailed, regardless that's not how you should hurt anyone. You should be glad TJ, considering the first thought I had, so can we please leave that alone…. Don't take me back to that place. You don't run anything, Deja. but we have some catching up to do. We'll see what happens.

Meanwhile

Bro MJ and RJ said they sent you a text, MJ said he tried calling you. Oh shit! My phone is at the house Damn it!! Let me ask you something Bro, what's up JJ what's on your mind, bro? What's going on with you and Trish not that it's any of my business but. So why you ask then? Oh, so you don't know what's going on! What are you talking about JJ, I don't know what! Well, let me show you. What the hell!! Who sent you that picture JJ? Our Lil' brothers MJ and RJ were out, and they saw Trish out with this guy. Oh, ok so that's what she wants to do ok Kool! But wait a minute that's the same guy that is next to Trish the same guy in every photo from her job, I recognize his face that's the guy! What happened with you two or should I not have asked? Well JJ me and Trish took a Lil break a few days ago it seems she's not wasting time to move on…. Well, I'll be Damn! Hey… what did you do TJ? Trish was nice! Bro like she flipped out on me a few days ago, I mean it came from out of nowhere. I came home from work early and she was already home. She went in on me about marriage and shit like that! It was almost like she had been programmed or something because I thought we were eye to eye about her picking a wedding date. She went off on me bro, so I've been back at my house ever since. I guess it's good your house never sold! Thank The Creator Right? But answer the question TJ you did something other than the shit that you're telling me. I'm your brother! Do you remember my ex, Deja? I do the lovely Ms. Deja, what's up with her so she's no longer missing? What the hell has she got to do with your current break with Trish? Well, if you shut the Fuck up and let me finish maybe you'll find out. Aww Damn TJ Why Do We Men Cheat! Because I know that's where you're headed. Come on bro if you don't know Why We Men Cheat just look around! We're here in the gym, look at how some of these women are dressed enticing, alluring and I get it some women really come to the gym and they're really about their workout and I admire that, but some of the women come the gym to hunt. They hunt TJ really! Of course, JJ there's this one woman that follows me all over this gym, I've spoken to her a few times, but she's seen me with Trish here many times, so she may think I would reject her if she was to go there. It's not always us men JJ, like you see what she's doing. She sees us here and this whole big entire big ass gym she wants to come do all these seductive stretches right here in our face, but soon as one of us says hello we're a predator. Am I right? I must agree with you there TJ. You know JJ there are more women than it is of us men, it's almost like one of them things, we should have an open invitation to the single women for things to balance out, and our significant other would just have to put up with it you know. If that was an ok thing, would that still be cheating? Funny TJ but you're right! Cheating is cheating though no matter how you put it! Well, it may just be better for us all. Damn right! Because women Cheat just as much as we men do and it's more women than it is of us men keep in mind again, I say! Ok, tell me why do you think she has that dildo stashed away as if you don't know about it? Where are you going with this? Ask yourself, why am I finding dildos and Shit in our home....

Tell me if you believe your wife is thinking about you sexually all the time of course we want to think so. News flash that's why the dildo is in her secret stash that's the cheating we are supposed to accept, who is she thinking about while she's getting down with the dildo? If she's not thinking about you, who is she thinking about...She is cheating on your dumb ass! That's why women say they're the better cheater. Shit, we men Cheat with the first nice booty or nice rack we see in the physical or by way of the internet LOL!! The somewhat trusty companion! And they're playing foul nowadays with this VPN business, I tell you they surely making it harder on us men today! This is why the olden days were the better days! I mean DAMN what do we do fellas!!! Deja made her appearance last Sunday morning me and Trish went to church service and who did I see... welp you guessed it, Deja. Oh, so you and Trish were together when you saw Deja TJ. Yes! So, it was the entry to a problem. I felt it, bro! Not in the Lord's house, don't tell me y'all went there TJ! Are you crazy bro.... there's no way I'll take it there! Well, you never know these days there's a video clip of a fight in a Church floating around now! Yeah, I know about it JJ. Yeah Pure ignorance! Long story short though Trish and Deja just so happen to be Colleagues now. What! Yeah, I know right... so Trish introduced me to Deja after Church service, so she thought it was an introduction anyway... and you remember I told you about the other day, I mentioned earlier about me getting off work early to Trish being home early as well and how ballistic she went on me. Yea, bro…Let me tell you! So, Trish invited Deja to have Sunday dinner with us. No way bro! Yes sir… she came and dined with us, she slipped her number and address to me. I never called her because I already had another issue going on, although I was curious about Deja and what Trish had told me about Deja not knowing who the father of her son is… I had to take the rest of this week off work and here I am. But you know something just doesn't add up JJ! Especially with how suddenly Trish came at me with all this marriage stuff! Well, you should know your mate, all I'm going to say is you better be careful bro. Last but surely not the least Deja is saying I'm the father to her son. Say what now! Yeah, you heard it right bro! Damn, bro well how old is he? He's 7 years old. So, wait a minute first of all she disappeared and now reappears with a child, and guess who's the Dad…. Bingo JJ! That's fucked up bro excuse my language…. Why would she hit you like that bro, they going to rip you apart with the back child support! Damn, I haven't even thought about that JJ. What are you going to do bro, if it was me… I'll be damn if she would think she could play on me like that, maybe she did leave you for your doggish and cheating ways, but oh no that shit just wouldn't fly with me at all! What are you going to do? Trust me I know what I'm doing. Hold on Lil' brother is calling. What's up JJ have you seen TJ? Me and RJ have been trying to reach him and we're not getting any answers. We done called that negro 50 times or more. Have you heard from him since we sent you those pictures earlier? He's right here with me now MJ. Put him on the phone. Hello. Man, we've been trying to get at you… Me and RJ bumped into Trish a little earlier! And she was walking with this guy with a rose in her hand smiling ear to ear, I guess he was giving her some "eargasms", so me and RJ confronted her. She told us that you two were taking a break or y'all have broken up or some shit! Well, we were taking a break, but damn like I told JJ, She isn't wasting any time hooking up with another man. Yeah, I see, and RJ was ready to put his hands on the dude! Well, I'm glad it turned out the way it did because the average man would've engaged with Trish, I mean she's beautiful from head to toe. He probably has no idea what me and Trish's status is. I hear you bro we were just trying to look out for you. I'm glad y'all did. Good looking out bro and I haven't answered my phone, because I forgot to grab it when I left home. Oh, ok because I was definitely about to ask you why you not answering our call. Well now you know MJ. I appreciate that again and I'll get back to you a little later. Alright, later TJ. RJ told me he wanted to put his hands on the dude when he started running off at the mouth. Well like I told MJ, I'm glad it didn't come to that JJ. Theirs No need for anybody to get hurt or killed behind another who will find another after you're dead and gone or locked up in prison for the rest of your life. Facts of life bro, I agree.

Meanwhile

Hello TJ, how are you, Babes? Hello Amber, how are you? I want to see you that's how I'm doing!! So, listen it is Taco Tuesday, and my mom and I do Taco Tuesday every Tuesday, but I told my mother that I would like to invite you to come over as well. Well, honestly, I do have some things I'm trying to take care of, and I saw all the missed calls, it wasn't personal, I forgot my phone at home when I left for the gym, and by the time I realized it I was putting my car in park at the gym! Oh, no worries, you don't have to explain because I know I haven't done anything except be a sweetheart to you! I must agree Amber, but I have some things to do I really do. Come on TJ pleaseeeee!! Besides my vacation starts tomorrow and I won't be back home till next Monday. I told my mother how you're such a nice talented man and we'll be glad to have you over just for some Tacos & Tequila! Alright Cool, I'm convinced what time are you talking? 7:00 or 7:30 will work for you babes? Please come on……… Please, please, please!!!!!!!!!! OK, I'll be their Amber. See you soon. Bye. Why did I agree to go over to Amber's place? Knowing I must get some issues satisfied. But I'm a man of my word. While cleaning up, I noticed some lingerie in my drawer. I knew they didn't belong to Trish; I knew who they belonged to. Deja is trying to play foul games, I feel it. Let me call her right now! She done started leaving belongings here already. Damn she not answering! I got to let her know about this shit. Oh, this must be her calling me back. Phone Ring, Hello. Hi stranger. Hi Lori, I hope all is well with you. I've been missing you; you know Divia suspended me? Yeah, I heard, Lori I have a question to ask you. What is your question baby? You do know you can have any man in the world, I'm sure I mentioned that to you once! You're so beautiful, you shouldn't be wasting your time on me. I can't lie you're super attractive super sexy super fun and if you were mine I would show you every day the love and passion I have for you. TJ let me tell you what I'm thinking. You know what never mind I'm just happy to hear your voice. I'm happy to hear from you too. You mean that TJ!! Yes, I do mean it. Do you think we can be more than friends? Well like I mentioned before you never can tell. I'll never say never. I just really think we'll be a beautiful couple TJ! I can't disagree Lori... Other couples would surely envy us. They surely will, because I would have what the other ladies want, and you would have what the other men would want. Can we talk later Lori I have some things to take care of, ok? Alright no problem, but TJ can you come see me later? Call me, but I can't give you a sure answer right now. Ok, I'm fine with that! I'll talk to you later Lori. Ok, honey. As beautiful as Lori is why is she content with wasting her time on me? I'm running late, I had gotten caught up talking to Lori, I thought I had gotten her out of my system. But not so fast. After all, I started thinking about the few days we shared and they were special, Lori knows how to reel me in and I'm just like the other men out here at times I get weak. Do I want to cheat? The answer is simply No, but a beautiful woman is worse than any drug or alcohol, because that woman will have you doing things that you say wouldn't do, That's a fact. Sometimes the standard isn't the standard for me. I can't say I understand what it's like to be a drug addict I can't say what it's like being an alcoholic. But I know the struggle of being a cheater and so do many others they just may not admit it. Hi there Amber. Hey, babes, this is my mother, Bella Jade. Bella Jade TJ. Nice to meet you! Bella Jade, you say. Yes, Bella Jade, but you can just call me Bella. Ok, no problem Mrs. Bella. So, TJ are you from North Carolina, Yes…. I grew up not too far from here. Amber told me some time ago she's from Texas. That's right TJ we're Texans through and true! But since we moved to North Carolina we love it here. Glad to have you for sure Mrs. Bella. What's that saying you all have in Texas? You must be talking about the…. All things are bigger in Texas saying. Yes, that's the one! Hmm, that's not all true TJ, because Amber's father had the smallest dick. Mother don't talk about my father like that!! Well, it's the truth! I didn't see that one coming… wow! Well TJ as you see my mother is a loose cannon she's extra feisty when she starts drinking Tequilla. Aww, I handle my drink well, I can drink you under a table. Not tonight, Mother,

I'm not going there with you! You have already gone there, Amber! I witnessed Amber and her Mother Bella Jade drink 5 straight tequila shots, I'm talking about the good strong Tequila but credit Bella because Amber tapped out. So, after we ate tacos, I had a few shots, but Amber knew I was going home, and I wasn't trying to get drunk. I must say Amber's mother is a fun person she's the life of the party. I mean nonstop Ambers's mom's motor was going nonstop she's electric LOL! TJ, can I ask you a question? Yes, no problem. Do you think my daughter Amber have a nice ass? Mother!!!Aww, hush girl! Yes, Amber has a nice plump booty. Let me ask you this, why is it that all of you black men love a big ass? Mom!!!! Lol, I can't speak for all of us, but I like the look, it is so sexy, and the feeling is very nice, and it looks so exotic when it waves… Hell even when you all walk it's a beautiful thing! I don't like an ass that's too big, some of us do though. Mmm-hmm, I see. TJ you don't have to answer my mother she done had one too many drinks! No, it's ok I don't mind besides she deserves to have her questions answered. Let her enjoy herself, Amber. Thank you TJ you know me and Amber were at the grocery store earlier and this guy was saying Damn they both got ass! He made it his business to keep walking by to look at me and my daughter's ass, I thought it was funny, cute even…Amber didn't think too much of him she just kept talking about TJ is this and TJ is that TJ-TJ- TJ…. I thought my daughter was going to make a damn song about you! Alright mother that's enough!!! TJ, let me ask you one last question and be honest ok!! Yes, mam Amber stand up and turn around Mom really! Now TJ you're a real man I know one when I see one….. Me and Amber are wearing nice fitting jeans as you can see, so be honest, which one of us has the nicer ass? TJ, you don't have to answer the question. Oh yes, he does come on TJ answer the question. Would you give me a pass if I break it down? Go for it. TJ, you don't have to do it, babe! By the way, that guy at the grocery store was Black. Lol, I know he was! I don't think I said that it's the tequila!! Well to be honest you're Ambers's Mother… No disrespect, you have a very nice bottom, but naturally, I'm going to say, Amber! Amber will get older, and she should only pray to have your figure, you wouldn't have any problems getting any man older or younger for sure. Are you happy now Mom? Not, completely. I heard you mentioned Amber's father earlier are you two still married? Lord!!! Not at all I caught him cheating with one of Amber's friends from college. Sorry to hear that. Come on TJ let's go to my room! You don't have to TJ if you don't want to, you can stay in here and keep me company. I'm going to go back there with your daughter excuse me nice to meet you, Ms. Bella Jade. Nice to meet you too TJ. Very nice! Thank you for being so nice to my mother. No problem at all. I don't know why my mom is always trying to compete with me ever since she and Dad divorced Bella Jade has been up under me, she needs to find her own damn boyfriend that's what she needs to do! And she wouldn't have any problems finding a man, your mother is very attractive! Thank you, TJ! I'm going to give you all of me babes… At this time, I had a few more tequila shots. Next thing you know we're going for the highest score, and I believe we reached it. I made her feel so good I put her ass to sleep. Now here's the crazy part when I got up and opened the door Bella Jade was on the floor with nothing but a thong on playing with herself. She got up off the floor and put her finger over my lips grabbed my hand walked me to the living room and she pushed me down to the couch! I tried standing up to make my way out of there, but she kept shushing me and pulling my dick out now keep in mind, I had just given Amber the Carolina Wood her daughter, and now here her mom is sucking me licking me you name it and I fail. I fucked Amber's mom good. Was it my intention not at all, I didn't want to go there, you can't say what you would've done if it never happened to you again I say. Was it planned… I don't think so and besides Bella Jade speaks her mind, I believe she would've said TJ I want to fuck you or something along those lines. I just believe she heard me giving the Carolina Wood to Amber and she got extremely hot and horny. One may say was it good…. Well, to be honest, I haven't had too many that were bad. You can call me every bad name that want to. But it's what I answer to. You can point the finger all you want to, but I promise there 3 more pointing back to you.

Love me or hate me, but you'll never break me. No one here on this earth can walk a fine line or be squeaky clean, It's NOT reality! if you can show me that person, then I can show you a horse doing jumping jacks. How dare any of you look down on me when you just fornicated reading what took place with me and Mrs. Bella Jade or should I say "Ms". Bella Jade. You "immature adults" are funny. You Know What! Goodnight. They wore me out tonight, but I held my own though fuck that shit. Lol sound familiar! If you know then you know. Come on in, hello to you! Teo this is your dad TJ. You're my dad? Well, your mom said you are my son so! Tell me Teo do you like pizza? Yes, it's my favorite! Well, I'm going to order us the best pizza they have alright. Awesome!! Can you tell them I want pepperoni and extra cheese? Whatever you want Teo. So, do you like it here in North Carolina? Yes, now I see my grandparents every day. You'll also be seeing me every day, how that sounds little guy! I would like that. TJ, I need to answer this call y'all excuse me for a second, I'm going to the ladies' room. Go ahead everything is fine! Me and Teo got this. Do you like sports? Do you have a favorite sport? Yes, my mom was looking at the team that wear Black and yellow colors. The Steelers so that's my favorite team. Nice! Yeah, she told me that is your favorite team! Yes, it is my favorite team your mom told you the truth there! Do you like school Teo? Yes, I love school! I have some nice Teachers. That's good to hear, well do you have a favorite subject? Well, I like math and numbers. Awesome Lil guy well here's our food it looks and smells good, doesn't it? Yes, I can't wait to eat it! Well, we going to pray over the food before we eat ok! Yes always.

Thank you, Lord

For this food, please let it be a blessing and nourishment to our souls, we thank you and Bless the hands that prepared this. Amen. Well, Teo let's eat! Your mom is still in the restroom, so we are going to start eating. Oh yeah. This pizza is good I like it! Enjoy it, little guy! Finally, you come to join us. Teo, we gone have to go after you finish that slice, ok baby? Yes, mom. Wait a minute... why are you leaving, I thought we were going to enjoy this evening together the 3 of us!! Well, something came up, and... And what Deja? Why are you acting so strange.... You know what never mind. You take off more than Delta. I heard that TJ. May we have a box, please? We'll talk later tell TJ bye and thanks for the pizza. Thanks, TJ bye. Bye Teo be good, ok? Ok, I will. I think it's coming back to me more clearly now why me and Deja broke up. I remember she started running towards the end of our relationship. It seemed as if she was hiding something. Now here she is again taking off something doesn't feel right. As I said she take off more than Delta.

But Why Men Cheat.

Hi TJ, I'm glad you decided to join us. Well, you are all here! I am at this grown and sexy event with the 3 ladies I met at the grocery store a few days ago, I called Stacey, and she told me to come hang out with them so let's see how it goes. We danced had drinks and just really enjoyed ourselves. Stacey, you're a firecracker for real, I mean I've never danced with 3 ladies altogether but hey it's a first time for everything right and you all are gorgeous you're all eye candy and a dinner plate. They all said thank you, and to be honest they're beautiful women… I mean why aren't they married I have no idea but wait just a minute let's see what happens next. As we sat down at this table, I've never had that much action going on at the same time well Stacey was holding my hand and Coi was rubbing her feet on my leg while Abella was winking at me, I never considered myself a playa, Mack, or pimp none of that shit, but the ladies truly crush on me one would say maybe it's the cologne one may say maybe it's my build one can and would say so many things, but it's one thing and that is my confidence. I feel I can have any woman in the world with my confidence! Surely you may not think so, but me and your girlfriend think I'm handsome! Again, I'm not being arrogant just confident. We all ended up leaving the club and we went to Stacey's home because we weren't ready to call it a night. After having some drinks, we all had very interesting conversations some good talk for sure, take a listen if you will. So, TJ did you enjoy yourself with us tonight? I did you all are a bunch of fun and have some good vibes! It was fun Stacey for sure. You know TJ when we met you the other day at the grocery, did it not intimidate you conversing with 3 powerful women? Well truthfully speaking Coi no not at all, I can handle it. I just so happen to be a powerful man! For which I will do my best you know. Because you do know we all talked about you said Abella. I'm sure y'all did as long as I gave you all something good to talk about... hey I done good for myself; would you not agree? I can't speak for them, but I do think you handled yourself quite well. Thank you, Abella. You know what's funny Abella is…. I just met a lady by the name of Bella yesterday. Oh yeah! I sure did. TJ, I felt you getting a bit excited while slow dancing if you know what I mean!! Oh, so you going to put that out there just like that huh Stacey? I don't see why not again we talk about everything ok! Like I said you're a firecracker Stacey dangerous even! And you would be right with what you just said there TJ. What do you mean Coi? TJ come back here with me for a minute. As I made my way to the back room well Stacey's bedroom, I couldn't help but think about what Coi was getting at. I think she may just be hating on Stacey a bit, why I don't know because if I had to pick, it would be a hard go, but it would probably be Coi, but then Abella looks good too... well, either way, one couldn't go wrong. Well, here I am again. Another fine mess I've gotten myself into. Some may not believe such action for a bro, but while into the action with Stacey... Coi and Abella came in and joined! A foursome!!!!! It was…. Awesome! I handled 3 beautiful ladies

89

at the same time oh what a night! I went home after a nice time with the ladies and oh by the way… The cologne I had on was English Laundry Signature Coi so now you know! It is confirmed because when I got back home the top was off…. again, I wear many fragrances. Now who would be calling me at this time of the night?

Hello

So how are you? Oh, look who decided to call me. Well, if it isn't Trisha Good what do you want? EWW…. By the way, I saw your brothers a few days ago. Ok…. so, I was told, I mean you wanted a break, right? You got what you wanted. You always do though, right? TJ listen I only said we need to take a break I never said we can't fix it; I mean we would have to try right? Why couldn't we have this kind of conversation a few days ago? It was no, no I want you to leave you remember that! Yes, I remember that although I had a few glasses of wine that day. Yeah, mid-day at that! Whatever TJ, but to be honest, I was angry at you when I thought about what Deja was saying to me at work. Ok, but why didn't you talk to me…. I'm your man right, why did you allow anyone to come in between us like that? I know, I know TJ, but I wasn't thinking, I felt a bit disrespected, Deja even had me feeling like a fool while talking to her! She had me so worked up TJ! Well, can you come check on the ole lady? I'm sorry. It would have to be tomorrow because I'm about to go to sleep. And besides I have something I need to talk to you about. Ok honey sounds good. And one more thing. Trish, do you remember when you showed me your company photos? Yeah, but that's been a good while ago TJ, but I remember, where are going with this? Well, that same guy that's in the pics next to you is the same fella that's in the pic my brothers sent me. I knew exactly who he was, is that not the same guy that was all close to you in every one of those photos from your employer? LOL yes. I told your ass years ago that guy liked you! Alright, alright yeah you did say that I agree! I know I did, and I was right Trish, but you know what else…. What TJ. It feels good to be right. Whatever dude goodnight. Lol…. You a trip! Goodnight. One of the first places cheating starts is at your employer. Ask me I'm qualified to speak on it and so are a lot of you. Truth be told you're probably agreeing with me right now, maybe. This cheating thing may be the last thing you want to hear. Again… I say, ask me I'm well qualified. But you know it's sad when you can't even embarrass a person, once upon a time you could, but not today. People don't give a damn today SMH. Hi, Coi how are you feeling on this nice afternoon? I'm, fine thanks for asking. No problem, you know I had a wonderful time with you and your friends. Yeah, about that…. Well, I should not have done you know what with you all. I let myself go and now I feel so bad TJ…. These were things I did in college, and it was only once, but here I am now a polished grown woman, and it was all because I

didn't want Stacey feeling like she had some power over me,
I knew when Abella went to the room I said to myself, they're
back to their old ways and I promise you! I didn't want to
go home.... I didn't want to sit up front by myself and be
lonely while I knew you all were back in the room enjoying
each other. You understand what I'm saying TJ. I hear you
loud and clear Coi, you know you should always go with
what your heart tells you. I mean I wouldn't have thought
any less of you if you hadn't joined us. I would've probably
respected you even more, so you know there's no need to
beat yourself down behind that. It's all good Coi, It's a thing
of the past now. We all do things that we later look back on
and say Damn what was I thinking! You surely have a point
there. I just wanted to talk to you about that, and one last
thing watch yourself with Stacey! Why would you say that
please do tell. No, I'd rather not. It's not my business to tell.
I can't speak on anyone's personal business you know what I
mean. However, I can tell you to watch yourself with Stacey. I
understand! It's just that, by you saying that makes me think
all kinds of things! Please understand. Like I said TJ, I don't
tell people business, but I can give a person a hint for which
I told you to watch yourself with her. I noticed you shaking
your head like is she serious a few times when Stacey was
talking... I'm going to be honest I thought you were low-key
hating on Stacey. Ha, ha me hating.... I don't think so! I also
said to myself Damn! Coi shouldn't have any reasons to be

hating, because she's beautiful! Thank you so much, but I have to get going, maybe you and I can get together soon. Only you and me though. I would like that Coi. Take care. On my way to Trish's house, I get a phone call from Amber and she's telling me how much fun it was on Taco Tuesday! She said her mother had another spark today. She said thank you for a wonderful night! I heard her mother Bella Jade in the background saying (hey Mr. TJ!) She must've said that 5 times or so. I responded by saying hello. Amber and Bella were at the airport getting ready to go to Miami for their vacation. Amber said I'll see you when I get back. Believe it or not, she wanted me to go with them, I told her I had too much to do, and I said I would see you when you get back. I hung up my phone and my phone rang again. I answered to hearing a voice saying Well, tonight is the night I'll make it alright...Just come over. I said no. She said underneath this skirt I have on a cherry red thong. But Damn I'll be wrong is what I said to myself knowing I should've kept driving to Trish's house I took another exit though. She said would you like to see. I said ugh no, knowing I was lying to myself. She said my fancy is wet, what are you gonna do about it I said nothing. She said you know you can have this fancy wet however which way you want it, I want you to hit it till the morning can you do that, She said my fancy is smelling like strawberries help me produce the cream lets make this dream reality again I'm so horny you can hit this fancy from

Carolina to California Stop tripping when you know you want this So, what you gonna do when the ass is phat and a chest to match, Know how to work the hips, The lips as well, Tell me don't you want to put that scented lotion on my plush bottom, Come back and do the same shit tomorrow, No strings attached tell me are you feeling that. I said no, no I'm gone got home and Trish's period on was on…Damn !! Dick hard aww the odd job. Got in the shower and thought about the plush bottom in a skirt in a matter of minutes I busted a nut. Well, now I guess I'm weak a little bitter all in all I'm a cheater.

Damn!

(TJ) get out of the shower, how you just going to come to my house and ask for the pot of gold and then go take a shower when I said no? I said exactly. Trish said exactly what! What are you talking about? I said Well I haven't seen you in a few days and since I couldn't have you in the physical I can and did in the mental. Let me tell you all something imagination is powerful as if you don't know that! But there I was lying my ass off knowing I stopped by Lori's house en route to Trish's house, but I stood strong knowing it truly took me a second to get up and run as fast as I could out of Lori's house. So, you see you may not say I'm guilty, but truly I was. I cheated regardless by thinking about Lori. To make matters worse, I was going to take it out on Trish for how bothered Lori had gotten me, but her friend stopped by to visit her…. So hey, blame me. I'm sorry about the way things went down a few days ago TJ. It's water under the bridge now lady, we must move forward Trish, but I have a confession to make. Alright, let's hear it TJ.

Phone ringing.

I'm 100% sure it's Lori Calling trying to get me to come back over so I was thinking. I'm sorry my bad with my phone anyway you won't like what I'm about to say! But.........Just say it TJ Damn!! Stop making me wait you're killing me here! Well to be honest I know Deja. YOU WHAT!!! Yeah, I know Deja, we used to date (many) years ago, and all of a sudden, She walked out of my life i never heard from or saw her until that day after Church. MOTHAFUCKER.... WHY didn't you tell me that SHIT that day... OH MY GOD..... Are you trying to kill me or something TJ!!! Of course, not Trish! Of course, not my ass negro!!!! Because I can taste the blood from the pressure... and I'm here to tell you somebody is about to get fucked up!!! How dare you!!!! WHY DIDN'T YOU TELL ME YOU kNOW THE BITCH!!! Trish, I gave Deja the benefit of the doubt.... She would tell you herself! But you're my man right TJ!!! Well, I was at the time! You surely didn't show it now, did you!! But you... A BUTT IS MY ASS DUDE! I'M NOT TRYING TO HEAR YOUR BULLSHIT FUCK YOU!! How can you explain yourself TJ? DAMN,, CAN YOU DO THAT? GO ON Explain!!!! Are you man enough to do that!! Trish, I explained that Deja and I had something going on once upon a time, and now she's saying I'm the father to her son. OH MY GOD!!! THIS GETS EVEN WORSE… I'm trying to see if I overreacted days ago, but you have made me change gears…. I'm at FUCKING TOP GEAR DEALING WITH YOUR ASS! My apologies Trish, I'm sorry I didn't tell you. That's why she was trying to put Charles in our conversation the other day at work. She had been trying hard to put Charles in every conversation we had! OH, CHARLES CRUSHING on you Trish… Charles this Charles that! Charles, Charles, Charles…Well, Trish, I bet you Charles can tell you about those actions from a man's perspective!!! AWW… TJ YOU LET THAT BITCH PLAY ON ME!! She told me that you didn't love me Trish… she said if she loved you TJ you guys would've been married. SHE PLAYED US BOTH TJ! CAN YOU NOT SEE THAT!! How do you figure she played us both Trish? I mean I do believe I'm her son's Father! I'm here to tell you that you're not! And you know this how Trish! Because the same day when I left work early, she left early, I guess she accidentally said, well I have to go about a paternity test with some guy and it wasn't TJ dumb ass!!! Oh, shit ok so she cheated on me when we were together, and I was excited thinking the child is mines! You know TJ, I think Deja forgot that she was talking to me when she mentioned the paternity shit. TJ what the fuck did you do to that BITCH! Trish, you have to believe me, I didn't even know she was pregnant, because she disappeared and left without saying anything to me... She told me she went and changed her number and she moved to Las Vegas. DAMN!!! Of all places where they really play games at!! Yeah, she FUCKED us both! You are right, I never thought about it that way Trish, games have been played! She said she got tired of me cheating and that's why she said that's why she chose to do what she did. Well, ain't that a …..Gone and say it "BITCH"! OH NO I GOT TO MAKE HER FEEL ME…. Have you seen the BITCH lately? I had pizza with her and my son. HE'S NOT YOUR SON TJ, I'M TELLING YOU DOH DOH DAMN! You haven't even taken one test…. Yet you claim the boy as if he's yours!! Ok, I agree but I just wanted to let her and him know that if I'm his dad no matter who I'm with, I would be there for him. RIVETING FASCINATING TJ…. HUH, WHAT THE FUCK EVER!! Come on let's go to your house… Like I said that BITCH got to feel it! She FUCKED up a Happy Home!! Oh yeah, she's got to feel it TJ!!! You know what come to think about it while out today with them, she had gotten a phone call she even went to the restroom for a while then all of a sudden, she came from the restroom all antsy, nervous even. I called her out on that. Like I said the boy isn't yours TJ.

Meanwhile

She tried calling me a little earlier. TJ call her back and tell her you need to see her, tell her to come over. Trish I was going to do that anyway but let me say there will be no violence. I mean really what would be solved if such action happened? Bhalzay Bhalzy Blah, just make the fucking call! Phone Ringing… Hey Deja I'm sorry I missed your call earlier. What are you doing? I just put the kids to sleep. How are your parents doing these days? They're fine, just as happy as can be having us back here in North Carolina. Well, that's nice, listen I need to see you Deja can you stop by? I can but only for a few and no sex OK. I just can't be doing those things with you anymore! Hey, it's no problem LOL…. I wasn't thinking of asking you for some ass… So, no worries, keep in mind you decided to reappear in my life. Aww TJ leave that tired shit alone as a matter of fact forget about all that has happened! Say what you can't be serious! Well, I am, and you know what never mind…. I'll be there in 15 minutes. Yeah, ok, Deja. Now you see that's why she needs her ass kicked TJ!! What she's trying to do is tell you that she won't be no longer seeing you anymore period. Little do she know; she surely will not be seeing you anymore. Doorbell Ringing…Hey there come in. Well, I'm not going to be too long so what's up… Just a second Deja, just what the fuck is your problem? One second, you're as sweet as can be then a few minutes go by and you're as sour as a Damn lemon! Topsy Turvy if you will… I mean are you Bipolar or something? So, when Shit doesn't go your way, somebody got to be Bipolar or whatever else you would try and diagnose someone with TJ. Well, let me tell you something TJ, Teo is not your son so yes, I cheated on you in our relationship. I'm sick to even call it that, but anyway hurt people hurt people right isn't that what you say all the time? You and that dizzy ass Trish... I broke you two up and I don't give a Damn I did both of you deserved it. OH, REALLY BITCH!! IS THAT RIGHT.... WHAT'S UP WITH ALL YOUR LIP SERVICE NOW? I SHOULD'VE KNOWN YOUR DIZZY ASS WAS HERE.... I tried to do you a favor by trying to hook you up with Charles because he wanted me, But I see TJ got you Fucked all up in the head!! SMACK.... I KNOW YOU DIDN'T PUT YOUR HANDS ON ME YOU SILLY ASS.... SMACK...LADIES' LADIES CUT IT OUT.... STOP IT .... Cut THIS SHIT OUT!!! GET YOUR HANDS OFF ME, TJ! AND BY THE WAY NO CALL NO SHOW YOU'RE FIRED BITCH!! I WAS QUITTING ANYWAY! THANKS FOR NOTHING!!! And take this cheap ass lingerie with you trying to mark your territory! You better be glad TJ is holding me back! You wish your ass could fill this sexy lingerie! YEAH, I see you walking on though!!!! Go run back to Vegas and play games with your ex-husband, because he got one up on you! Don't you want to go back to settle the score with him? Girl stop wasting that hot stinking ass breath!! I bet you won't get your ass out of the car Deja... Yeah, Bye Bitch! Come on back in the house Trish. Trish what are you doing!!! That Bitch gave me the finger. I swear I wish that rock would've hit her car!

Just come on in the house Trish it's all over now. Do you want to spend the night here with me tonight or.... No, take me home TJ! I need some time to myself.

Meanwhile

After the storm was over, I started hanging out with Stacey 2 or 3 days a week, we were having such a great time together, I mean she would come to my house, I would go to her house, and we would have sex all throughout each other house. We were mostly at her house though. So, one day she said TJ don't just stop by today without reaching out to me first. I had no problems with that, I mean she was the one that said just stop by whenever you want to. That's how comfortable she was with me. I know my situation was a bit different so she would call me whenever she came over to my place. Well anyway, Stacey knew what to say and how to say it to get me to her nesting. So, I called her to see if it was all good for me to come to see her and she said yes of course. While there on that evening we were getting it on like I mentioned earlier, we were sexing all over the house from the kitchen to the garage and I would spend the night sometimes. I would be there 2 to 3 days straight so later on that night we got into action again, but while doing the nasty my phone must've rang 40 or 50 times back to back, I looked at the phone and I didn't recognize the number so I kept getting the goods Stacey was producing! And on that night, it felt as if I was having a champion night, normally I would grab a shower, but on that night, something told me negro get out of there! Leave from out of that house right now! So, I told Stacy I was going to go home because I had a lot to do early in the morning. Stacey said you just want to know who was calling you back-to-back. Stacey said Well it doesn't matter because I gave you a workout tonight, so you're completely satisfied anyway. I agreed with her and got my ass out of there! As soon as I got in my car, I called that number back. I thought it was probably one of my brothers or family or friends who didn't have anything to do but play on my phone. Not at all though, I never seen that number… So, I called, and A guy answered and said Hey ugh TJ, is it? He said listen here that house you just came out of is my house. I paused and said who is this? I started calling off family and friends names. The guy on the phone said you don't know me but let me tell you something …. I Pulled over in a store parking lot, He said I thought about killing you tonight. He said Stacey is my fiancé, he went on to say Coi gave him my number, and he said I'm a long-distance truck driver. He started crying he said I do everything for Stacey. He said sometimes when he came off the road Stacey wouldn't even want to touch him, he said, I want to put you down I swear…. I swear I do. He said Coi told him that it was all Stacey doing. He said that Coi said Stacey never mentioned me to you at all! He said Brother, I'm hurt, he said Why do Men Cheat in a loud voice!!! He said it's not your fault though!!! You did what any other man would do looking at the beauty of Stacey. I said Hey man my apologies to you, I told him, I'm not into breaking up a Happy Home. I told him he never has to worry about me ever again hooking up with Stacey. I gave that man my word and ever since I've held strong to my word. I said Hey man I know you love her because, to cry to another man I can only imagine your pain. Respect! I went on to say I gave you my word and may The Creator Bless You. Some women play foul and dangerous games, I mean here this guy knows what I look like knows what kind of car I drive, and I have no idea if this dude could be standing next to me and want to carry out what he is feeling. I don't know what he looks like. talking about an ugly situation well there you go, if only Coi told me. But it got crazier …. Check this out, keep reading!

End Call.

Believe this or not the very next day Stacey asked me to come over and make her feel good. I cussed her out and said Don't you ever in your life call me again and I hung up the phone on her. Later I received a text that said I got my eye on you P.S. Admirer. As one can see cheating is an ongoing thing. But let's UNLOCK the reason Why Men Cheat… Follow me!

THE END

OUTRO

In closing all of us are similar but there are some differences, I mean even twins are different. I don't have all the answers, but it's a tough job for us all and none of us have it all figured out. It doesn't matter how poor or rich, it doesn't matter your race all mankind. You know with the phone call from that long-distance truck driver when he cried telling me how hurt he was, he had to be a strong guy. Because I can only imagine if it was me…. And then his lady reached out to me the very next day, I mean who does that? The first thing I thought about was that Meerkat when he caught his lady cheating. The Meerkat didn't want anything to do with his lady anymore and she had his kids she had mothered his kids. They were a family. The truck driver didn't even have kids and he was willing to hang in there with the one that hurt him. Salute to him. I'm simply explaining the similarities between us men the male gene if you will, you saw where the male Meerkat sent his cheater packing. But the trucker wants to work out the issues with his lady and there's nothing wrong with that. Love is strong, love is rare today, so if you have it Cherish it. One can't call him weak. Just like the Meerkat one thing we don't know is how many times he took his lady back to where he said ENOUGH. I can't take any more you have to go. Why do Men Cheat huh? We all have our reasons. I say there's only ONE REASON. You would know more better than me when it comes to us men cheating if you have asked all of us men around the world and surely, we all will give you an answer, every one of us would come up with various reasons, but truly there's only one. If you didn't pick up the reason why cheating can come about in the storyline, I advise you to read the book again instead of always just looking for an answer. People listen, it can't come from an argument, it can't come from seeing your mate too much, well there goes your relationship anyway, correct? I've heard many reasons I even used to come up with reasons myself when I was younger, I'm a grown-ass man now though! It had to be something that sparked your interest let's start there. Question yourself why I am asking Why Men Cheat. See what you may come up with. If you find your answer and you know the answer talk to your mate, it doesn't mean he's going to stop his behavior of cheating. If we're at this point, it's too late the damage is done. The question is then.... Do you stay or do you go, because we all have been a fool a time or two and this applies to all. Experience is a good teacher you know... No matter what a lot of you may say you too are a cheater, if you dreamed that freaky dream and it wasn't your mate well, you're guilty. If you fantasize about another girl if only for a second you had lust in your eye, you're a cheater, no matter how you may try and spin it. I really advise you to read the book again and concentrate on every detail.

If we going simply off a reason… How many people do you know that always say their New Year resolution is to lose weight they say this every year, and honestly have you seen any results? I credit the ones that stay firm, this doesn't apply to you. Now ask yourself for an example you're on a diet, you're trying to get your body right, you're trying your best to be at your best, but you see a commercial and on this advertisement, you see that steak and baked potato I mean the juicy steak sizzling and so you start thinking about the seasoning and how it smells you start thinking about the cut of the steak albeit T-Bone, Filet Mignon, Porter House whichever one that satisfy your pilot and then there's the baked potato with that melted butter and cheese, bacon the chives and all… You know you got to put a little salt and pepper on it, for it must be flavored right? This is from your favorite restaurant, your new year's resolution, you say the same thing every year and then you look up and you see the same damn weight or more that you were a year ago, I know somebody out there is agreeing with me right now! if not you're the same one eating the steak and baked potato and saying the same shit at the end of the year big as a house! What I'm saying is you were

"Tempted" to go and get that steak dinner. So, you see.... to all of you around the world the root cause of cheating is Temptation. UNLOCKED

"TEMPTATION"

That's why We Men Cheat. If there's anything that leads us to cheating, it's that smoking hot body she has! It's either we've had it and we want it again or we want it because we never had it and looks good!!!! Harsh Reality. The booty the boobs the beauty, the three B's. Booty, Boobs, Beauty. Hey, it gets us every time it will forever be on the menu. Could there be anything else NOPE!!! Not at all. This is just confirmation for some of you. If you don't know by now cheating is a revolving door that will forever spin around. Hey, don't blame me, that's just life for some. For many should I say and if anyone says and see it differently.... Where was your mate last night?

Thank you all
for reading "Why Men Cheat", I hope
you all enjoyed this book, I really enjoyed
sharing it with you all.
May The Creator Bless You All
Toris Jones

Man Cave

Fellas you remember when you were young a younging running wild? LOL! Wait a second… I heard that somewhere before! Another one of my favorite Rap Artist. One of the greats! He hails from Queens bridge, yeah that's him. He had ether for lyrics! It shouldn't be hard to tell! He only needed one mic! Anyway, America and the entire world. When I was a young boy, I shared a room with my older brother. Our room was our territory, so we thought. My older brother used to have some places he would hide things at so would I! Dirty magazines dirty movies you name it. Back in the day, we would say get out of my room if someone was found in there. So many times, I wanted to say that to my Dad! But I was smart enough to say that. Get out my room!!! Not in real time anyway! My dad didn't play that. One would be very brave to say such words to my dad. Get out of my room! Off goes your head LOL! But seriously though, he believes that long as you stayed under his roof. It was his way or the highway. Respect in other words is what we demanded. I can't blame him. That's what is wrong with kids today "No

Respect" for their elders. But that's another book. when it come to home space, we fellas can forget about it... That is if you're married, or you your girlfriend live together. A five-bedroom house with no children to sleep in not one those rooms. For the fact you only get a Lil space in the closet for your clothes. Your lady has clothes flooded everywhere in the closet. I'm not going to mention bed space... Let me just say... How does a petit woman take up all the space in the bed albeit a Queen or King size? Somebody right now knows what I'm talking about! I know I have more than one witness, hey, well it's better than sleeping on the couch or resting with one eye up LOL. Anyway, the place you call home is your castle. In this home you should be entitled to your chill out relax room, pool table, poker, movie, music, art whatever you desire this room to be. We fellas can talk all we want about this room and what we going to do to decorate it. If that woman has something to do with it... Not so fast Fella!! That woman wants to know what you're putting in that room. What are you doing in that room. Who are you talking to in that room Who's allowed in that room. What you can and you can't eat in that room. Can't fall asleep in that room, why are you spending most of the time in that room. Why do it smell the way it smells in the room. I know you're not talking about me in this room, who are you on the phone with!!! You hear me ... who are you talking to!! My parents' babe Damn!!! Oh, tell your parents I said hello.

Then they walk off still talking yap, yap, yap! My uncle told me and my brothers and my other cousins... we men can't live with and without the ladies.

I remember that same uncle I just mentioned passing words with his wife at a family reunion! His wife said, "you know what T you make me sick"!!My uncle responded, but it was super ugly what he said, well it was funny in real time. He said Well since I make you sick... "Die and prove it"! Woo.... That's cold blooded but being married well over 35 to 40+ years entitle you two to say some ugly things here & there. At the end of the day, you're going to kiss & make up & move on. Well nine times out of ten. Ugh... well I hope so anyway. What's the color of love? "Red" The bloodline everyone should have love, I did say "should" now. We all bleed trough similar veins. That's the one thing we all have in common, yet hatred is still at large.

SMH!!!!

When it comes to hide outs there aren't any! Sorry to be the bearer of bad news. Listen! Even when you think you're not being watched, you're being watched, facts! Yes, that's right someone is always watching. First, you should know The Creator see all. Facts! So, we may pull one on our significant other, but we won't slip one by the big man Facts! I had a friend of mines to tell me that he had been messing around on his wife. He said TJ, I have done some stupid things in my days of being married! But he said, by far cheating in his home with the mistress was the dumbest. facts! I couldn't agree more. He said TJ, the Temptation was too great. He said he didn't want to do it, but he fail and found himself getting it on even in him & his wife bedroom. Cheating is foul as is! But in the house… Play stupid games win stupid prizes. In your bedroom where your wife also make love to you & the rest her eyes at! Damn that's crazy suicidal you ask me! I said to him…You wasn't thinking at all. He said T let me tell you something. I done so many things to please my wife. You name it brother I did it. He said TJ tell me something. "What do women want"! He said my wife "complained" about her employer, so I told her to quit & look for another job. He said, she did everything but look for another job. He said months went by & she wouldn't even fix him a hot plate. He says bro she wouldn't even clean the house when she was there just sitting on her ass! He said, but she talked & gossiped on her phone then asked what we are eating today as if she's had a long day at work. He said TJ, I still loved her to the point where I was going out of my way to pay bills & she was concerned about me buying her wigs & purchasing clothes for her. He said I would go into the bedroom thinking I'm going to get a Lil loving, but she would complain until one day he said he went into his man cave & started looking at xxx flick & started gunning off to it. he said the T.V. volume was loud. He said he did it purposely. He said his lady walked in & caught him in action & had the nerve to cuss as if he was wrong. He said I gunned off looking at porno because I didn't want to go & hook up with another woman while being married. Why Men Cheat? Really!!! He said all the years I invested with my wife, he said she became lazy & made it as if I owed her or something. Then had the nerve to talk about me years ago when I was laid off, he said she never tried to build him up, but Moreso tore him down. Talking about Acrimony. He said when my back itched, I needed her to scratch it, but it was wishful thinking. He said TJ you got answers tell me why our sisters feel we owe them something! I saw he was frustrated & upset, but really, I had no answers. Well, I did but, took me a Lil while to think about that one. For I'm still thinking abut that one. SMH... But read while I share with you all with his permission the rest of the story. He said, I'm at the point of, I don't care anymore, he said I was ready to move on. He says he told her they weren't working out & he wanted a divorce. He said that's how the whole thing ended up him messing around cheating all in the house. He said she was mad as the devil, but she didn't want to divorce. She continuously made it as if he was the only one wrong. She didn't think she had flaws & faults. So, he said I continued on doing what I was doing and who I was doing it with. Then he said he stopped for a couple of months trying yet again to salvage their marriage. Until he saw his wife slumber back into her ways again. So, he says

I went back to doing you know what with you know who only this time, he said I didn't want to go into the master bedroom with such action but ended up getting it on in the man cave. He said what he didn't know was his wife went & had cameras installed without his consent. Wow! I know right Wow!!! Let me just say it was a nasty divorce, I'm sure one would agree. Foul is foul, but sometime or another you have to leave well enough alone. Fire surely burns. In the end she ended up with just about everything & to me I think that's foul. He said she screaming & yelling talking saying stuff like (& with white bitch)! Excuse me while I say this!! But does it matter what race they are when one has been exploited cheating? Hell no! It shouldn't … Damage has been done! "I'm" sorry to say this, I'm going to apologize in how this going to sound. Ladies keep this in mind… pussy is pink when opened up. Then again, I'm not sorry for saying that because, that's good old man talk. I love y'all though! Fellas keep that in mind about the cameras being installed ok. I'm not saying cheat either! Hey ladies don't blame me for your cheating ass boyfriend or husband. It should occur to you to check yourself because maybe you were the reason why he went & cheated. You know what's going on in your home & if you don't, just maybe you're being cheated on. Harsh reality. I'm signing off from the Man Cave LOL. I told my buddy I think she planned the whole thing what are your thoughts somebody?

Happy Home

It's a beautiful thing to go home & you're received with love. There's nothing like it. it's a sweet feeling. What I'm talking about go somewhere & stay for a while even on vacation. Something about home I tell you. A happy home that is! I've heard the saying home is what you make it facts! If you're married or single this applies to all. You just got paid, rent is due. The realtor company have given an extension on your last month rent that wasn't paid. You have a family at home & before you go & take care of home first, you go to the rim shop & pay off your balance, so they can put the rims back on your vehicle. Let me just say STUPID! Damn you're stupid! What about your family? Oh, I get it!!! you just had to have the rims! How the hell can you explain that to your significant other? That's money spent you dumb ass! You had corruption in the house last month, because you couldn't pay your rent. Why people cheat? Now here you are yet again can't pay your rent! Why people cheat? Hey, but your ride is looking good though. Yeah right! You are an idiot!! Why people cheat? The holy bible say man can't live off bread alone that's the Lord words. Facts. And your significant other has been bringing in the loaves of bread minus the meat because, she can't do it all dummy! She needs your help & vice versa ladies! You all want to get that expensive bag & instead of calling & checking in to see if it's in the budget you make the $800 Purchase also STUPID! A dumb selfish ass move was made! Why men cheat? Let's just call it what it is!! I'm not sugar coating anything that is dumb. I'm not justifying your dumbness. Dumb +dumb= 2 Dummies, I say that, because in relationships we take on one anthers personality. Facts! For an example… Hey babe let's go get that S550 Benz! I was thinking the same thing sweetheart! Two great minds think alike. Continue to read… Well, were you able to get the loan? They didn't give me all I was looking to get, because I still have something I need to pay off on my credit. Well, the car salesman said bring him $5,000 down & he can put you in the car! You have all the money now so… Let's go get the car! Yeah, Let's do it sweetheart! Baby I'm going to look good in that Benz! I couldn't agree more sweetheart. You get the car & your car payments are $698.00 a month.

Your rent is $1600 a month then you factor in the rest of your bills plus the $3,500 loan you just took out to purchase the vehicle… Oops my apologies the S550 stupid ass! you have to pay interest on the loan as well & you are bringing in a Lil bit over $2,400 a month. Really… SMH. How are you going to afford to drive the car? Then what about the maintenance on that car, ooo wee! You're smart I tell you smart. But you got the Benz. Yeah right!! One thing for sure you can't fix stupid facts! I get it! you want to spoil yourself, but that goes with common sense. Wake up people! These are the same people that will tell you that your dreams are unaligned & you need to stop dreaming. No don't listen to that, because people like that are called dream thieves. Let me just say this! "If you can't Dream, you're still sleeping". Be what you inspire to be. The Lord said in the Holy Bible!!! If a man thinks it so, is he. There shouldn't be no roof to successful heights. So, the couple have the S550 Benz, they stay in a apartment, but why get that kind of car staying in a apartment complex that have no garage? SMH… That's not disrespecting people that live in apartment complexes, I'm talking about the ones that do the dumb things like the couple I just written about. Get it how you live that also goes with common sense. I will say this, young people will & is going to do things that they will later say when they get older if they get older… Damn what was I thinking! I know, I been there and done that. Preventive action prevents actions. All facts! For the greater good we have to do better, but get out of all the illusions you see. Theirs a set back & a set up which one are you? I have a tattoo that read T2. The underline read judge not 2 day, 2morrow never. The T2 simply means Toris 2day, because 2morrow never waits. And if one still can't understand where

I'm going with this, they're the ones in the set back. The hardheaded never learn, let me also mention… A dream is void if action isn't put forward. Like faith is the unknown the unseen, but believing it's something greater if I keep going! Facts! Now since the S550 have been repossessed…The colors will fly then. The conversation may sound like this now. Remember I said a couple take on each personality! Listen to this here. Honey why were you two months behind on the car payments? Well, there are other bills right! Right!! But… But nothing!!! I need to catch up on the payments & that's it! well there's no need to be mad at me! Don't try to make it out to be that I'm the reason the car got repoed! Well, you were riding in the car! Oh, are you serious now!!

Why would you go & get the car if you knew it was going to be hard for you to afford? That's all I want to know! Leave me the fuck alone before I say something I'll regret later on woman!! Whatever and you aren't crazy either! Nobody didn't tell your ass to go & get that damn car! You better watch how you talk to me! You better watch how you talk to me! You better watch how you fucking talk to me, shit!! Talking to me as if I'm a child! What you need to do is get your shit together!! That's what the hell you need to do! You won't saying that shit when you were driving the damn car! And now I got to go get my shit together ha, ha you funny lady! So now I got to get my shit together because my car got repoed! Maybe if you help me out a bit more, I would be able to keep some shit!! Well, don't blame me, dude!!! You know I don't like where I work so!!! Don't even go there! Well, if you don't like your situation change it! But don't sink a ship that I'm trying to keep above water. But I need to get my shit together... you need to think before you speak lady! I need someone to love me fully, not just because I make more money & I can live a sweeter life minus 40 earned hours of your own. Whatever dude What The Fuck Ever!

Why Men Cheat?

Now when it comes to a couple that have their stuff together. They are what I call a power couple. Now this couple will not go & do the same thing the last couple I talked about will go & do. They are more concerned about retirement & equity in the home, vacations, and health and surely, they are not going to argue about a car or vehicle oh no no! The car or cars they have, they've had for years. And the cars still fire right up as if it's new. You almost have to beg them to go & get a new vehicle. Talk about driving it until the wheels fall off... well there you go! So, for example... listen to this couple and how they go about car shopping. Baby, yes honey! So, I was just watching this commercial about the new S550 Mercedes. Ok & what about it honey? Have you seen the new one babe, do you like it or not? I like the car! I think it's nice hun! Why you ask babe? Well, baby, I'm thinking about going to the dealership & take a look at a few of them possibly test drive one. What do you think sweetie? Ok so only to test drive one babe? Why not just get it if you like it, babe? Well, I will only if it's good on gas. They do have those good motors babe. True. Well, let's just see what happens.

You are approved for the car! Do you like the one you test-drove, or would you like to build one to your specifications? I would like to build one to my specifications. A few weeks pass by and the new S550 is beautiful. Friends & family stop by the couple's home & they see the car in the driveway. They think it's someone else car because they all know how frugal the couple is. It's good to know your better half is your backbone, but when making certain purchases one shouldn't rely on the other. Why? Well, you just read about the last couple that went & got the S550 Mercedes. When it's all said & done the last guy had to do so many things to get the car. He had 1,500 in the bank that he took out to make the 3,500 loan meet $5,000. Red flag if you have to go & take out a loan to get a vehicle, simply you can't afford that vehicle. One may say! Well, he mentioned if his lady helped him out, he would be able to keep some goods. Still wrong! Because if your income doesn't add up you best stand down, point black period. The time simply wasn't right. Just because a car salesman says he can do this & he can do that well he or she is just doing their job. Commission! Hey, a sucker is born every day! Besides his lady doesn't even like her employer hint, hint not too many of us do! And if he lost goods being in the relationship with that woman. He should've known making a huge purchase like that would come to bite him. If you can't build up each other in a relationship it will soon come to an end. It doesn't matter if it's an interracial relationship or not. So, let's not even go there! Love sometimes means, you go this way & I'm going to go that way. If it's real & true love & in The Creator's plans, not yours, you'll be back together. And you could then be that power couple that happy couple if you will! So, ladies, you were that dicknotized or fellas to pussytized to see the bad habits from you're your mates. No! what you thought was you could change that person & it blew up in your face when it was all over. Sometimes a good idea should stay just that, a good idea. People should be who they are! Don't hide who you are for no one. If you're sorry you're just sorry you don't need one to tell you what you already know. But a lot of people put on masks in relationships creating fantasies being Hollywood no, no bump that for you know who you are there shouldn't be no fabrication. Now you have your soul mate in tears saying I didn't know you were an alcoholic babe! You simply avoided seeing him with a beer in one hand & a shot of liquor not once but the entire first date. Really! Or what about you lady? Telling your Girlfriends all your business that goes in your house even down to your man dick-size girl he only got 10 inches. He still can't satisfy me. Well sweetie it isn't the size of the hammer it's the nail you're throwing it at. Maybe you can't be satisfied due to the sex addiction. 10 inches in & out of your sugar walls for a good 5 to 10 years sweetheart! Maybe your walls aren't so sugary these days, I'm simply saying let's stop justifying things for your greater good. Go & seek help in other words. And if that person loves you, they'll show it by being there. Let's stop surprising our better halves with tears & pain, lies, and disrespect. What makes a happy home is love. Like waking up for church on Sunday morning. You two are getting dressed happy as can be because you two know The Creator has been good to you both. Blessed! You return home from church just in time for your 1:00 football game. Your lady asks you, what you want for Sunday dinner. She goes into the kitchen, and you hear those pots and pans & you smell the spices and herbs & your team has just scored a touchdown. Your lady comes into the room & brings you your drink of choice along with some snacks until dinner is served. You have taken off your suit & she's undressed & have put on comfy clothes as well. You are flying your team colors she is as well & you two are laid back on your couch in your man cave enjoying home. Your lady gets up to check on the food that she's cooking on the stove. Every time that she walks by you spank that big ass booty of hers! She loves you & you love her. You two share everything, there's no secret in the house. But the reality is reality nobody's perfect. Now dinner is being served. You go & prepare to eat. You're so hungry... The snacks you ate a little earlier were just a warmup preliminary if you will. Now it's time for the main event! You rather eat your food in the man cave, because you don't want to miss not one snap of that nail-biting game! You bless the food before you start eating. You bite into the chicken breast & your significant other notice the face you're making while chewing the chicken breast. She asks if there is anything wrong with the chicken breast. You say, babe, you put a little too much seasoning in the chicken breast. It's a bit too salty. Now watch how a happy home erupts! Too salty huh? Well, fix it yourself the next time! You didn't help me do a damn thing! You just went in the man cave set on your ass & watched the damn game! Babe, I'm just saying it's a little salty that's all. I didn't say I wasn't going to finish it but... But nothing! Go find yourself a chef from now on! Because you always have something to say about my cooking!

You don't appreciate me!! Baby yes, I do appreciate all you so! I was just trying to tell you... I know what you were trying to say! You've already said it so leave it the hell alone and go buy yourself some dinner get the hell up from the table & go look at that dumb ass game!!! I must say if that is the only problem you have at home you have nothing to worry about. I can assure you long as you're in a relationship, arguments are sure to come. Go get that woman some roses & a cookbook. Make some good love. That's a happy home! Ladies just like y'all need us we need y'all as well. We all need The Creator! Ladies be our better half without the stress & mess it's only but so much we men can take. Therefore, you wouldn't have to ask the Question.

Why Men Cheat.

Thanks again,

Author,

Toris Jones

Why Men Cheat? Why Men Cheat was
written in 2018. Refreshed 2024

This was my story love it or hate it. I enjoyed sharing it with you all.

"Why Women Cheat"? "Home Wrecker Diaries". "REVENGE" "The Power Behind The Throne" "The Black Silk Comics" Coming Soon. Also stop by www.whymencheat. com website and podcast. Thanks for your support. Toris Jones By; Toris Jones

Wait just a minute all! I interviewed some men & asked them, Why Men Cheat! Let's see what they had to say. The conclusion to "Why Men Cheat".

Name:

Sleazy Vegas

Age	Marital Status	Profession	Annual
39	S	Lab, Scientist	$ N/A

? Why Men Cheat.

We men are not attracted to what we thought was a natural beautiful woman. You later find out she wears the mask when we all know the mask is to be worn on Halloween. So, isn't that like a game in the beginning? But yet the women want to call us out about games. But when you look at it, makeup is a game. Changing Faces… It's a game that some of us men are unaware of. The woman simply isn't the same woman you thought she was when you met her. You were attracted to a facade.

Name:	Age	Marital Status	Profession	Annual
Zay	22	S	Lab Logistics	$55,950

? Why Men Cheat

Being young & inexperienced how can a man be serious? A young man such as myself lol! So, for example, I met my lady at a young age & I feel the chemistry is there, but temptation is the root cause of cheating. Like you said TJ.

Name:	Age	Marital Status	Profession	Annual
Loose Chains	48	S	Doctor	$198,990

? Why Men Cheat.

We men get tired of getting accused of cheating. You've or should I say, we men have been cheated on & heartbroken. We men cheat to see if we still have it. Then there's the "Pussy Punishment" women come & hit us men with! Women will cut us off from getting the coochie. SMH! Sometimes we men get tired of the same woman.

Name	Age	Marital Status	Profession	Annual
The Goat	35	S	N/A	$110,000

? Why Men Cheat.

Cause we're dogs, Woof, Woof, Woof and the cat won't let the dog get it!

Name:	Age	Marital Status	Profession	Annual
Iron Addict	34	S	model	$85,950

? Why Men Cheat.

When your woman is not paying you any attention. That is a Red Flag & it would lead to cheating. She has pushed one to go & cheat. For example, when I ask my lady over & over, let's go out on the town & she refuses constantly. That alone forces a man to cheat.

Name:	Age	Marital Status	Profession	Annual
Minister	46	M	Coordinator	$98,980

? Why Men Cheat.

A ton of reasons, you can chase the wrong one, and you end up with the lady you didn't want. How can a man approach the right one? We men are sensitive. We play a hard role, we're built differently, and you feel lost without no love & no lovemaking. Hey, our need definitely must have attention. So, if the needs aren't addressed, we men have been forced to cheat. The attention isn't the same from the beginning. Attention will come one way or the other. There are so many of us that, are corrupted due to our wants & needs. It can be an ongoing affair when bedroom action isn't happening. The more women call us dogs, the more they need to ask themselves, why am I calling this man a dog? By the way, King Solomon had many wives because he had great needs.

Name	Age	Marital Status	Profession	Annual
Biggie Bang, Big T Love Jones TJ	40	Single/in a relationship	Lab Specialist Ceo: Exq 1	N/A $86, 574

Why Men Cheat

?

It all starts in the King James Holy Bible, in the book of "Genesis". Yes, the beginning. The Adam and Eve story. Understand Adam was told not to eat from the tree of knowledge of good and evil., he was told not to eat fruit from the tree in the middle of the garden, and he must not touch it. God commanded Adam and Adam failed by doing what God told him not to do. He "Adam" fail by being tempted by "Eve". So honestly, we men who walk this earth will never pass the test of cheating. If one thinks about it, we men are cursed when it comes to women. Keep in mind the serpent was also on the tree of knowledge. The serpent is the devil. It doesn't matter how beautiful your girlfriend, or your wife is, one will always rival you. It doesn't matter what you do sexually and how well you may treat your man, ladies, for we men will fail solely by "Temptation" and this concludes "Why Men Cheat". It is written in the Bible, that even if a man thinks it, or looks at another woman with lust he's guilty. The word is not to be debated.

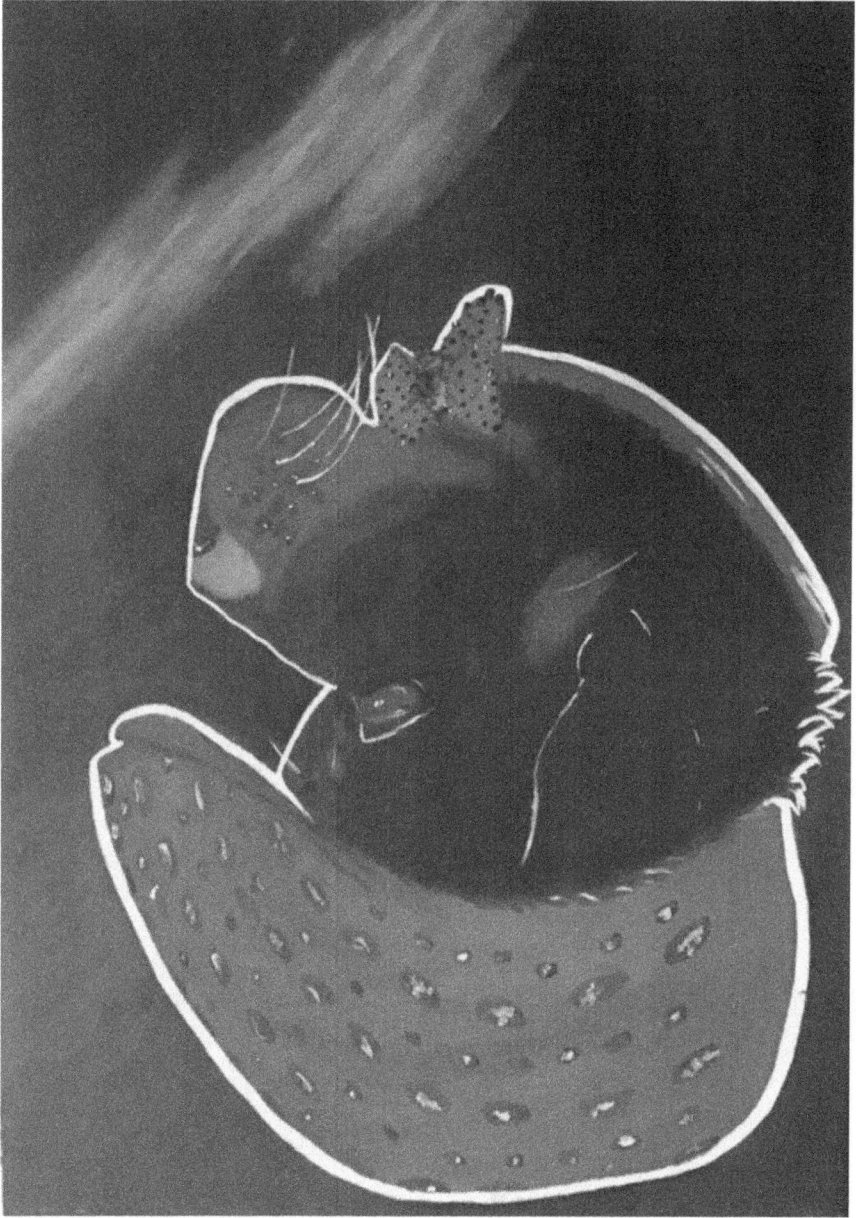

Thanks For Stopping by Be Sure And Give Your Lady A Life Time Supply Of Carolina Wood! Supplying The Ladies 365! If You Know, You Know.

Attn: All Men Around The World You Too Are A Supplier Of Carolina Wood.

You Can't Go Giving Acres To All The Ladies Choose Correctly.

You've Been Warned!

TimberRRRRRRRRR!!!
I approved this message.
Tori Jones